Railway Track Diagrams

Book 1:
Scotland & Isle of Man

Edited by Gerald Jacobs

TRACKmaps

1st Edition 1987
2nd Edition 1993
3rd Edition 1996
4th Edition 2001

ISBN 978-0-9549866-3-6

©Trackmaps 2007

Published by Trackmaps, Little Court, Upper South Wraxall, Bradford on Avon BA15 2SE
Tel: 0845 300 1370 Fax: 0845 300 1375
Web: www.trackmaps.co.uk Email: sales@trackmaps.co.uk

Edited by Gerald Jacobs   Original Cartography by John Yonge

Digital Conversion & Design by ESR Cartography Ltd   Printed by Polestar Wheatons (UK) Ltd,
Woodley, Reading RG5 3LE   Exeter EX2 8RP

Railway Track Diagrams
Book 1: Scotland & Isle of Man

Editor: Gerald Jacobs

Preface to the Fifth Edition

This edition of the Quail Track Diagram for Scotland represents a milestone. It is 20 years since John Yonge of the Quail Map Co published the first edition which was to prove the fore-runner of country-wide coverage and updated later publications.

The very first edition was drawn in 1987 by John from a combination of industrial sources, previous "survey" trips and a holiday taken "riding the rails" with paper and pencil in hand, using a week long travel pass. The concept was strengthened when Gerald Jacobs as editor joined forces with John as cartographer and publisher, putting their combined knowledge and the attention to detail into full and effective practice. The resulting series of books in 5 titles and various editions has provided a reference to Enthusiasts and Industry alike and contains information which may exist elsewhere and in other forms but is unique in making it all available in easily portable volumes.

In 2004, Trackmaps took over the publication of these volumes and embarked on the digital conversion of the information, incorporating updates at same time. With the publication of this Book 1, only one of the 5 titles in the series remains to be converted.

The series covers the entire UK mainland network on the basis of the original British Rail regions and includes private railways and London Underground. The network is covered roughly on the basis of the original British Rail regions. The information included is a combination of historical sources collected by Gerald Jacobs during his 40 years with British Railways, added to subsequently, kept up to date with reference to Network Rail and supplemented by other data, by the kind assistance of other persons and by field observation. This Book was last updated in 2001 and represents a tremendous amount of work in catching up the intervening years.

TRACKmaps, December 2007

Introduction

The Track Diagrams in this book cover the lines forming the Scotland Route of Network Rail, together with a small part of LNW Route and a number of private railways and industrial layouts. They are, in general, up to date as at December 2007.

However, records are wonderful things. They can both inform and confuse. Nowhere is this more certain than on the UK Railway Network. Built up, as it has been, over more than 180 years, managed as individual companies, as a nationalised industry and now as individual train operating companies with a single infrastructure owner, it has grown, stagnated, declined and grown again more than once within that time. Many persons have produced records and maps at different times for different parts, both within the industry and outside. Many record systems compete for information or act in a complementary manner to each other. Track Diagrams attempt to collate these diverse sources into one publication but, even so, space precludes the inclusion of much detail including, for example, signals.

Track Diagrams also try to put down a standard where discrepancies occur; mileages are typical. Mileages often vary slightly between different official records but, in general, those given in Sectional Appendix have been used. Station mileages are usually taken from the mid-point of the platforms or, in the case of a terminus, the buffer stops. The Railway is continually changing and, because of its diverse nature and varied history, discrepancies often arise between seeming accurate sources. In such circumstances, the Editor's judgement is applied.

Acknowledgements

A large number of people have contributed to the information in this publication, some in a significant way providing layouts, site checking or proofing details and some in a small way giving personal observations, answering individual questions or giving access to engineering drawings and construction diagrams. The assistance of all is gratefully acknowledged, especially persons at Network Rail. Other contributing individuals include persons at EWS Railways, together with Iain Scotchman, Michael Oakley and Simon Lowe. Other acknowledgements are due to the Branch Line Society, the Railway Correspondence & Travel Society and many other correspondents, other railway societies and also representatives of the private and preserved systems featured.

The Editor is indebted to Peter Scott for details of certain private and preserved railways (see also his website http://web.ukonline.co.uk/pe.scott/index.htm) and to Ewan Crawford for valuable reference material and photographs on his website, http://www.railscot.co.uk.

The digital production of this book could not have proceeded without the efforts of the team at ESR Cartography Ltd but special thanks must also be given to two people; firstly, to John Yonge, the originator of the track diagram artwork, whose cartography and advice provided a sound basis of the maps in the book; and, secondly, to Elvina Jacobs for her forbearance and continuous support given throughout the Editor's long and arduous task.

Gerald Jacobs

KEY

————	Running Line
————	Siding
————	Electrified overhead
————	Electrified 3rd rail
————	Electrified 3rd rail (Underail contact, DLR)
————	Electrified 4th rail (LU)
————	Electrified, overhead & Conductor rail

A broken line indicates 'in situ' but out of use, proposed or under construction.

——•——	Line obstructed
——○——	Line out of use
——⋮——	Change of Signalling mandate
LNW ‖ SC	Network Rail Territory boundary
Motherwell ∣ Glasgow (M) (G)	Signal Box / approximate area limits
—)--(—	Tunnel
≈	Bridge under Railway or Viaduct
—⅄—	Selected Motorway / Trunk Road bridges over railway
—╁—	Network Rail operated level crossing (or LC on other than NR lines)
—¦—	User-worked crossing with Telephone [NT] indicates no telephone
←——←	Track signalled in both directions (a double arrow indicates normal direction of travel) (On single lines 'DN' indicates down direction)
←——→	Wrong direction of travel
—⋈—	Private siding boundary, often marked by a gate
——⅃	Sand Drag
—⊘—	Turntable
⋯⋯⋯⋯	Gantry Rails (Freightliner Terminal)
wwwwwww	Wall / Bank / Fence
—▲—	Hot Axle Box Detector (HABD), Wheel Impact Load Detector (WILD) or Wheelchex Device

ECM	ELR-Engineer's Line Reference (Prefix and suffix numbers indicate sub-divisions and their boundaries)
[SC 147]	Line of Route Code
∣ 93	Whole mileposts, shown on the appropriate side of the line
∣ 32	Whole kilometre posts
81.3⌉	End of mileage run
$\frac{54.50}{69.67}$ COM	Change of Lineside mileage
•	Location Spot for mileage reference
3	Platform with number (May be supplemented by sub-divisions. e.g. (a), (b), (c), 'N' or North etc)
⑦	Indicates number of carriages per platform (approx 20m lengths, the actual number may be less to accomodate operational restrictions)
⬚	Provisional proposed platform
▭	Former Royal Mail platform
▭	Platform out of use
⏍	Other feature (labelled)
▨	Loading bank
Glasgow (G) ⊠	Signal Box or Signalling Centre, with code (underlined text relates to SB or SC)
⧄	Control Panel
⧆	Gate Box
□ ⊙	Ground Frame/Ground Switch Panel or Shunting Frame. ⓈIndicates 'Shut in' facility
⊛	Radio electronic token block / Token exchange p• and No Signaller Token with Remote crossing Lo•
¶	Proposed closure
○	Water tower or column
∧ ∨ ⊤ ⊤	Significant changes in gradient; summit trough and others
(Seafield) •	Indicates location spot for a former Jn, Station or Signal Box
86.34 (Not italic if Station mileage)	Distance in Miles and chains from specified zero 1 Mile = 1760 yards / 1.6km 80 chains = 1 Mile 1 chain = 22 yards / 20.11m
57.60 km	Distance in Kilometres

Guide references are given to pre-nationalisation, pre-grouping and sometimes pioneer railways e.g. LNE : NB (Edinburgh and Glasgow)

Traditional Line Descriptions may be quoted, e.g. WEST COAST MAIN LINE

Publisher's Note

Every effort has been made by the editor to ensure the accuracy of the information in the book is as correct as possible at the time of going to press. Notwithstanding, the Publishers welcome corrections, updates or suggestions for application to future editions

GENERAL ABBREVIATIONS

AA	Acid Application	ft	Feet	Qy	Query concerning distances etc, unresolved
ABP	Associated British Ports	GB	Gate Box	REC	Reception
AC	Alternating Current	GC	Gantry Crane	RETB	Radio Electronic Token Block
ARR	Arrival	GDS	Goods	REV	Reversing or Reversible line
ASC	Area Signalling Centre i/c IECC, Power Box	GF	Ground Frame	RR	Run-Round
bdy	boundary	GL	Goods Loop	RT	Railtrack
BCH	Branch	GS	Goods Shed	S	South
BR	British Rail	GSP	Ground Switch Panel	S & T	Signal & Telegraph
CCTV	Closed Circuit Television	H	Headshunt	SB	Signal Box or Southbound
CET	Controlled Emission Toilet Discharge	HABD	Hot Axle Box Detector	SC	Signalling Centre
CL	Crossing Loop on Single Line	HH	Hopper House	SCC	Signalling Control Centre
COM	Change of Lineside Mileage	HST	High Speed Train	Sdg(s)	Siding(s)
CR	Cripple Siding	IECC	Integrated Electronic Control Centre	SD	Sand Drag
CW	Carriage Washer	Jn	Junction	SF	Shunting Frame
C&W	Carriage & Wagon	Jt	Joint	SIMBIDS	Simplified Bi-Directional Signalling
D	Connections Disconnected	km	kilometres	SN	Shunt Neck
DA	Down Avoiding	L	Wheel Lathe	SP	Switch Panel
DC	Direct Current	LC	Level Crossing (manned, automatic or open)	SS	Shunt Spur
DE	Down Electric			TA	Tamper Siding
DED	Diesel Electric Depot	LHS	Locomotive Holding Siding	TB	Turnback Siding
DEP	Departure	LP	Loop	TEP	Token Exchange Point
DF	Down Fast	LPG	Liquified petroleum gas	TL	Traffic Lights
DG	Down Goods	LS	Locomotive Shed	TMD	Traction Maintenance Depot
DGL	Down Goods Loop	LW	Locomotive Washer	T&RSMD	Traction & Rolling Stock Maintenance Depot
DL	Down Loop	M	Middle		
DM	Down Main	M ch	Miles and Chains	TS	Through Siding
DMD	Diesel Maintenance Depot	M&EE	Mechanical & Electrical Engineer	U&D	Up & Down
DMUD	Diesel Multiple Unit Depot	MGR	'Merry-go-round'	UA	Up Avoiding
DN	Down	MN	Main	UE	Up Electric
DPL	Down Passenger Loop	MOD	Ministry of Defence	UF	Up Fast
DR	Down Relief	MU	Maintenance Unit	UFN	Until Further Notice
DRS	Down Refuge Sidings	N	North	UG	Up Goods
DS	Down Slow	n	not electrified	UGL	Up Goods Loop
DSB	Down Suburban	NB	Northbound	UH	Unloading Hopper
DT	Down Through	NIRU	Not in regular use	UL	Up Loop
E	East	NR	Network Rail	UM	Up Main
e	electrified	NT	No Telephone provided	UPL	Up Passenger Loop
EB	Eastbound	OHC	Overhead Crane	UR	Up Relief
EGF	Emergency Ground Frame	OLE	Overhead Line Equipment	URS	Up Refuge Siding
EMD	Electric Maintenance Depot	OOU	Out of Use	US	Up Slow
EMUD	Electric Multiple Unit Depot	ONS	Overhead Neutral Section	USB	Up Suburban
Engrs	Engineers' Sidings	OTM	On-track Maintenance	UT	Up Through
EoL	End of Line	P	Points padlocked	V or Vdct	Viaduct
ESP	Emergency Signalling Panel	PAD	Prefabricated Assembly Depot	W	West
EWS	English Welsh & Scottish Railway Ltd	PL	Passenger Loop	WB	Westbound or Weighbridge
	Fence across track	PS	Private Siding	WD	War Department or Wheelchex Device
FA	Flushing Apron	PSB	Power Signal Box	WILD	Wheel Impact Load Detector
FP	Fuelling Point or Footpath	PW	Permanent Way	yds	yards

SUPPLEMENTARY ABBREVIATIONS FOR THIS BOOK

Cal	former Caledonian Railway	LNW	former London and North Western Railway
ER	former Eastern Region of BR	LMR	former London Midland Region of BR
GB&K Jt	former Glasgow, Barrhead and Kilmarnock Jt	Mid	former Midland Railway
GNofS	former Great North of Scotland Railway	NB	former North British Railway
GSW	former Glasgow & South Western Railway	NE	former North Eastern Railway
High	former Highland Railway	NER	former North Eastern Region of BR
LMS	former London Midland and Scottish Railway	ScR	former Scottish Region of BR
LNE	former London and North Eastern Railway		

LEVEL CROSSING ABBREVIATIONS

STANDARD	Supplementary	Description	STANDARD	Supplementary	Description
(ABCL) *		Automatic Barrier Crossing, road warning lights and barriers monitored by Traincrew		(MWLG)	Miniature Warning Lights with Gates
(AHBC) *		Automatic Half-Barrier Crossing		(MWLO)	Miniature Warning Lights at Open crossing
(AOCL) *		Automatic Open Crossing, road warning lights and barriers monitored by Traincrew	(OC)	(O) (OPEN)	Open Crossing (non-automatic), without barriers, gates or road traffic signals
	(AOCR)	Automatic Open Crossing, Remotely monitored	(RC)		Remotely Controlled manned Level Crossing (gates) operated locally by Signaller or Crossing Keeper
	(BW)	Bridle Way			
(CCTV)		Manned Level Crossing (full barriers) with Closed Circuit Television operated by a Signaller or Crossing Keeper	(R/G)		Miniature Red and Green warning lights i/c Miniature Stop Lights operated by approaching trains
	(FP (B)(G)(K)(W))	Footpath crossing (only shown if telephone provided) (B) Barriers, (G) Gates, (K) Kissing Gate, (W) Wickets	(TMO)		Traincrew Operated crossing
				(TMOB)	Traincrew Operated Barrier
(MB)	(MCB)	Manned Level Crossing (barriers) operated locally by Signaller or Crossing Keeper		(TMOG)	Traincrew Operated Gates
	(MCBR)	Manned Level Crossing with Barriers, Remotely controlled	(UWC)	(UWCP)	User-Worked Crossing of occupation, accommodation or bridleway status with telephone except where noted as [NT]
(MG)	(MCG)	Manned Level Crossing (gates) operated locally by Signaller or Crossing Keeper		(UWB)	User-Worked Barriers
	(MGH)	Manned Gates, Hand worked		(UWCM)	User-Worked Crossing with miniature Red and Green warning lights
	(MGW)	Manned Gates with Wickets			
	(MSL (B)(F)(G))	Miniature Stop Light with (B) Barriers, (F) Footpath, (G) Gates		(UWG)	User-Worked Gates
	(MWL)	Miniature Warning Lights		(UWK)	User-Worked with Kissing Gates
	(MWLB)	Miniature Warning Lights with Barriers		(UWS)	User-Worked Stile
	(MWLF)	Miniature Warning Lights at user-worked Footpath		(UWW)	User-Worked Wickets
			(WL)		Barrow or Foot Crossing with White Light indicators

X) shown after these abbreviations e.g. (AHBC-X) indicates that the crossing works automatically for movements in the wrong direction.

In some cases, the code of the controlling signal box may be shown e.g. (AHBC-X) (KS)

If no abbreviation is shown, the level crossing is either operated locally by a Signaller or Crossing Keeper or privately but equipped with a telephone.

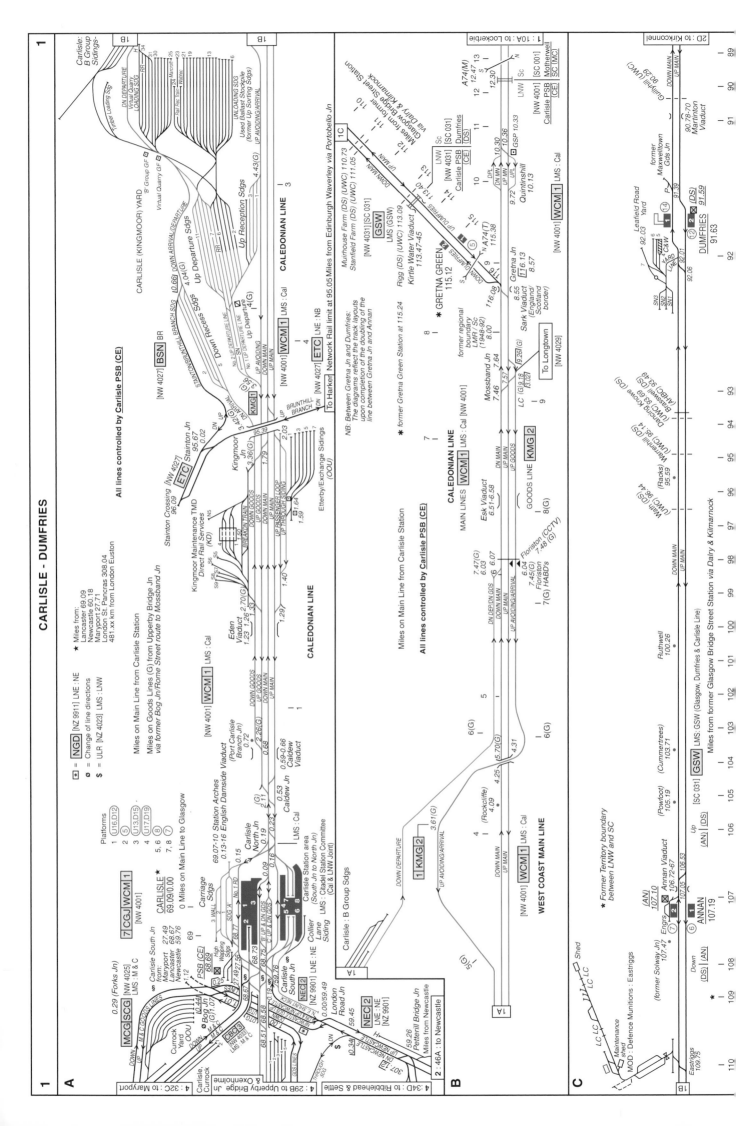

CARLISLE - DUMFRIES

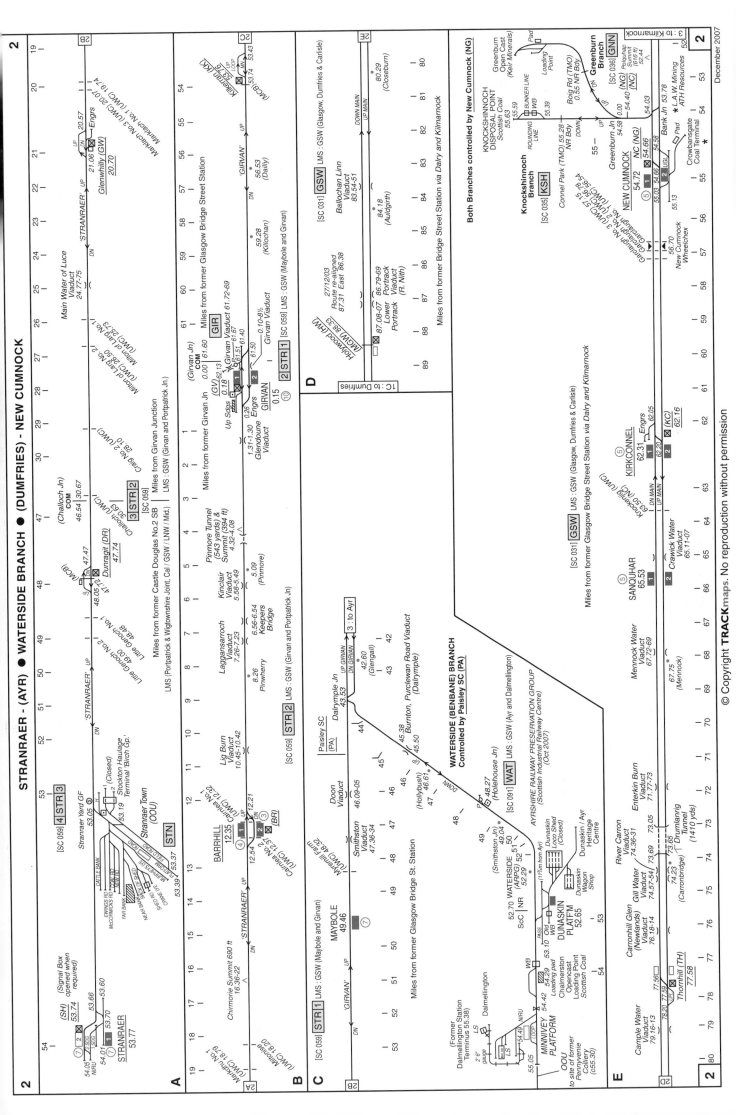

STRANRAER - (AYR) ● WATERSIDE BRANCH ● (DUMFRIES) - NEW CUMNOCK

December 2007

© Copyright TRACKmaps. No reproduction without permission

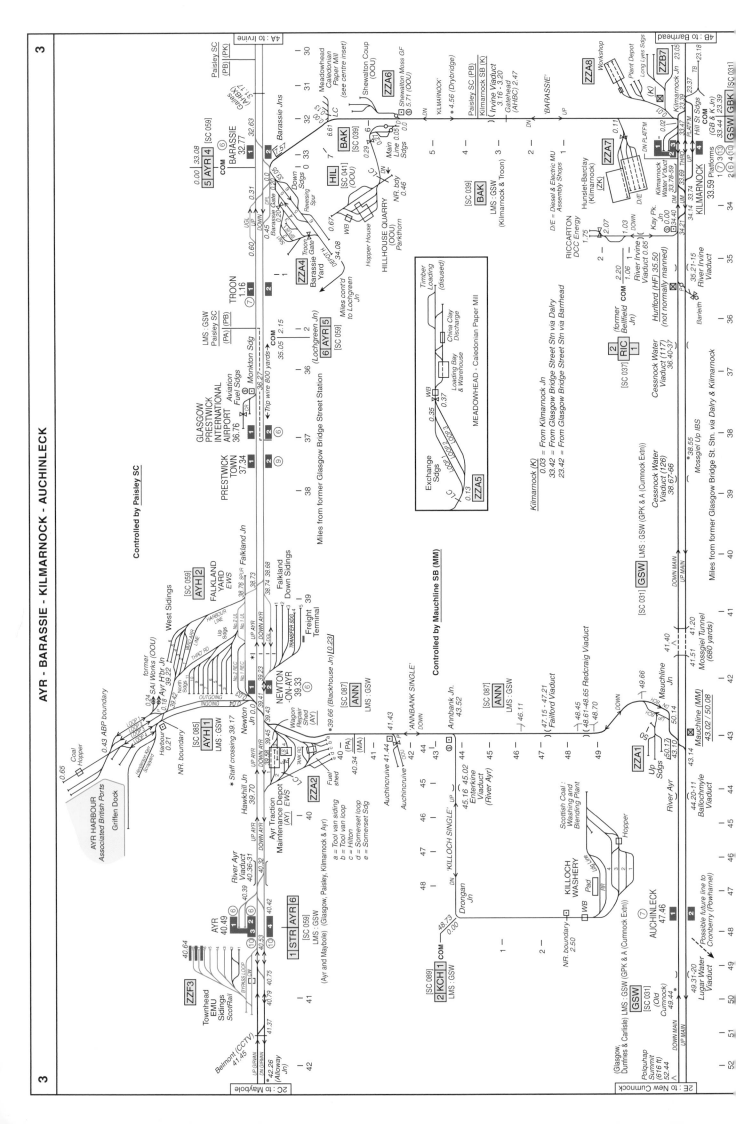

AYR - BARASSIE - KILMARNOCK - AUCHINLECK

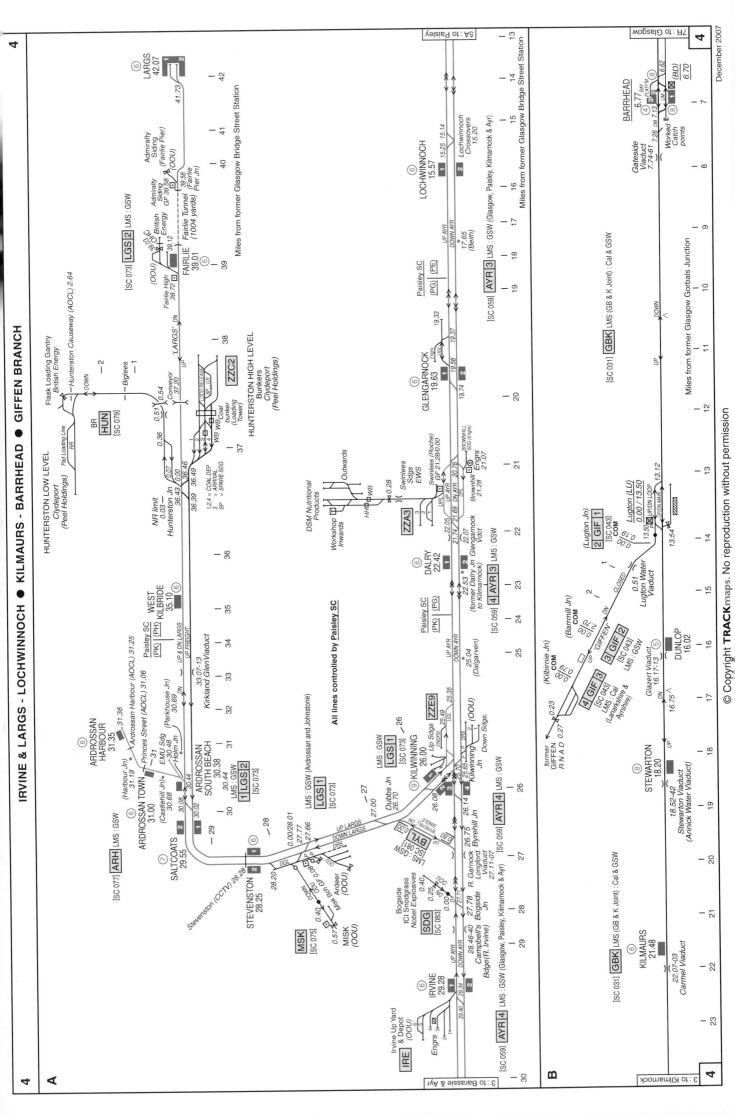

IRVINE & LARGS - LOCHWINNOCH ● KILMAURS - BARRHEAD ● GIFFEN BRANCH

December 2007

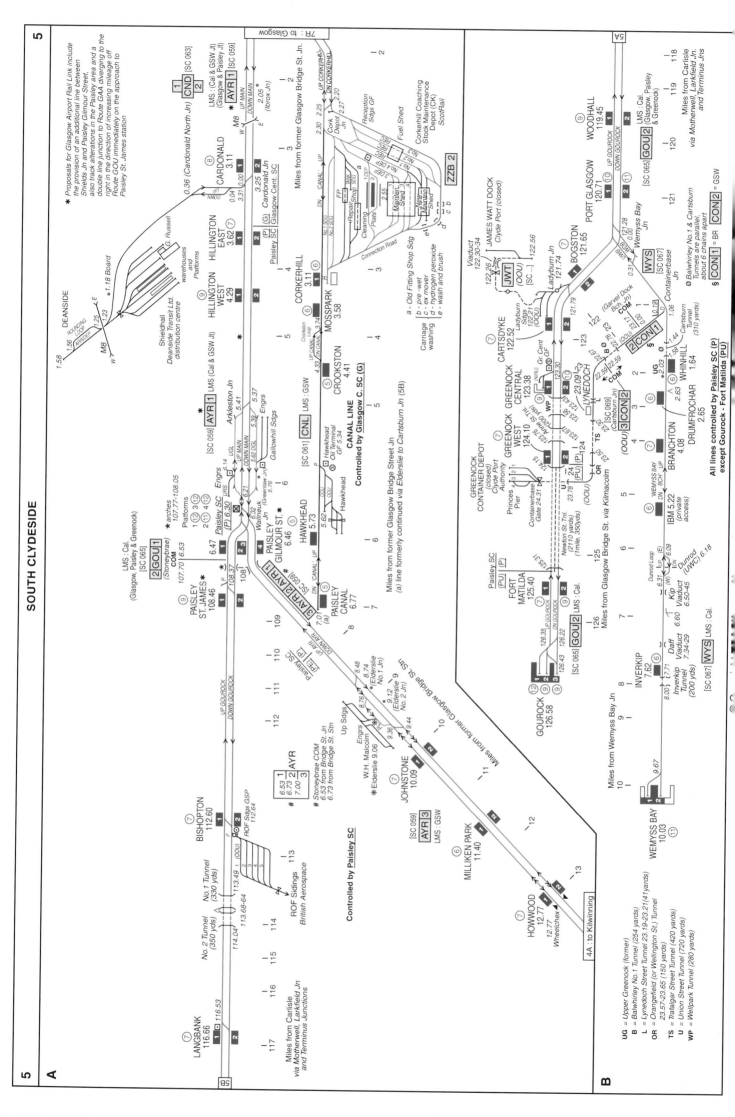

SOUTH CLYDESIDE

NORTH CLYDESIDE

A

7L : to Milngavie

WESTERTON
6.10

7L : to Glasgow

7L : to Glasgow Queen St. HL
via Maryhill

| Miles from Glasgow Queen St. HL
via Maryhill

(YY) (YH)
Yoker SC

6.20 6.19 (6) **1** ► **2**
6.16 6.19

Westerton Jn.

SCOTSTOUNHILL
1.20 (7)

DRUMCHAPEL
7.20 (6) **1**

(YY) (YH)
Yoker SC

2 (8)

A North Yard line
B South Yard line
C West end crossover
D Centre crossover
E East end crossover

East End
1.67

GARSCADDEN
1.58 (6) **1 2**

| 7

| 8

[SC 123] NEM5 LNE (NB)

DRUMRY
8.10 (7) **1**

2

[SC 125] YKR LNE : NB (Clydebank Loop)

East H. 0.0

M.P. 1.70

Stabling
Sidings

EAST
Sidings

11
12
13
14

E

15
16
17

Cleaning
Sidings

18
19
20
21
22

WASHER LINE 2.33

REC

D 2.15

CW

A

C

B 0.00 0.28
*Rothesay
Dock Sdg*

REC 2.40

HDEP

DEP

1
2
3
4
5
6
7
8
9
10

WEST
Sidings

West End
2.43

YOKER
2.56 (8) **1**

2

Yoker SC (IECC)
(Integrated Electronic Control Centre)
2.04 ⊠

YOKER CARRIAGE SERVICING
DEPOT (YO)
(electric multiple units)
ScotRail

| Miles from Glasgow High St.
via Hyndland

UP SINGER
DOWN SINGER

8.48
(Singer Works Jn)

UP YOKER
DOWN YOKER

SINGER
9.05 (9) **1**

2

*Dalmuir
Tunnel No. 25
(90 yards)*

*Dalmuir Twin
Tunnels No. 23
(110 yards)*

CLYDEBANK
3.43 (9) **1**

2

UP YOKER
DOWN YOKER

3.60
D

*Clydebank
Riverside Junction*

0.00
COM

◄LMS : Cal. **BR** LNE : NB►

0.04

109.05

2 RVS 1

[SC 139]

Platforms
1, 2, 3 (7) (6)
4, 5

DALMUIR
4.62 **4** (6)

3
2 1

4.53 4.40
4.36
4.25

UP YOKER
*RIVERSIDE
(OOU)*

4.20 YKR
LNE : NB

[SC 125]

DN & UP

Erskine Bridge 11.13

4.73 10.01
DN SDG

*Dalmuir
Park Jn* 9.71

*Dalmuir
Riverside*
109.52

109.49

109.28

*Clydebank
Riverside Junction*

| Miles from Carlisle
*via Rutherglen and
Glasgow Central (LL)*

| Miles from Glasgow Queen Street High Level
via Maryhill

KILPATRICK
11.17 (6) **1**

(7) **2**

All lines controlled by Yoker SC

Yoker SC
(YD) (YY)

BOWLING
12.70 **1**

2

*Bowling
(CCTV)* 12.78

13.07

(6) NEM 5
[SC 123]
COM
(Dunglass Jn)

LMS : Cal LNE : NB

113.46 13.40
(Carlisle) *(Queen St.)*

| Miles from Carlisle
*via Rutherglen,
Glasgow Central (Low Level)
and Old Kilpatrick*

UP HELENSBURGH
DOWN HELENSBURGH

| 114

| 115

6B

B

BALLOCH
20.38 20.35 (6)

20 —

ALEXANDRIA
19.20 (6)

19 —

RENTON
18.11 (7)

18 —

17 —

*'BALLOCH
BRANCH'*

7 NEM 6
[SC 123]
COM
(Dumbarton East Jn)

15.51 116.00

(Miles from Glasgow Queen St. (HL)
via Maryhill)

←(Miles from Carlisle via
Rutherglen and
Glasgow Central (LL)
and Old Kilpatrick)

[SC 135] BCH

LMS : Cal & LNE : NB
Dumbarton & Balloch Jt.

DN *UP*

16.69

UP BALLOCH
DN BALLOCH

16.38 16.31-25
*Leven
Viaduct
No. 77*

DALREOCH
16.35 (7) **1**

2

*Dalreoch
Jn.*

DUMBARTON
CENTRAL
16.08 (9) **1**

16.16

2

16.19

DUMBARTON EAST
115.59 (8) **1 2**

15.24
(Leven Shipyard Jn)

15.73
15.66

DPL

*Loading
bank*

*High Bank
Sdg. GF* Ⓖ
16.05

High Bank
Sdgs

ZZF2

(N/RU)

Engrs
Sdgs

(EMERG)

15.51

6A

| 115

Miles from Carlisle

LMS : Cal. LNE : NB

LNE : NB

LMS : Cal. & LNE : NB
Dumbarton & Balloch Jt.

| 17

17.04

*Dalreoch Tunnels
(550 yards)*

16.59

| 18

17.04

UP HELENSBURGH
DOWN HELENSBURGH

18½

[SC 123] NEM 7
Yoker SC (YC) (YD)

| 19

| 20

CARDROSS
19.50 (8) **1**

(7) **2**

*Geilston Farm
(UWC)* 20.29

19.55 (CCTV)

20.07 20.29

*Geilston
(UWC)*

*Brookes Farm
(UWC)* 20.49

| 21

*Ardmore East
(A1BCK? X)* 21.18

*Moss Road
(UWC)* 21.75

| 22

Craigendoran Jn

22.76 -0.01
-0.18 -22.58
WH

0.6 DOWN

WWWW
sea wall

H = HELENSBURGH LINE
WH = WEST HIGHLAND LINE

[SC 141] WHL

NEM 7
[SC 123]

| 23

CRAIGENDORAN
23.18 (8)

DN & UP

24.17 24.10 'HELENSBURGH'

*WEST
HIGHLAND*

DN & UP

**Controlled by
Banavie SC (RETB)** | **Controlled by
Yoker SC (YC)**

HELENSBURGH
UPPER
2.08 (7) ✳

| 2

| 3.70
(Rhu)

*Ardencaple
(UWC)* 3.17

2.52 (UWC)
Woodend

HELENSBURGH
CENTRAL
24.31 (10) (9)

3
2 1

(9)

Miles from Glasgow Queen Street High Level
via Cowlairs & Maryhill

| 24

NEM 7
[SC 123]

21A : to Gairlochhead

© Copyright **TRACK**maps. No reproduction without permission

December 2007

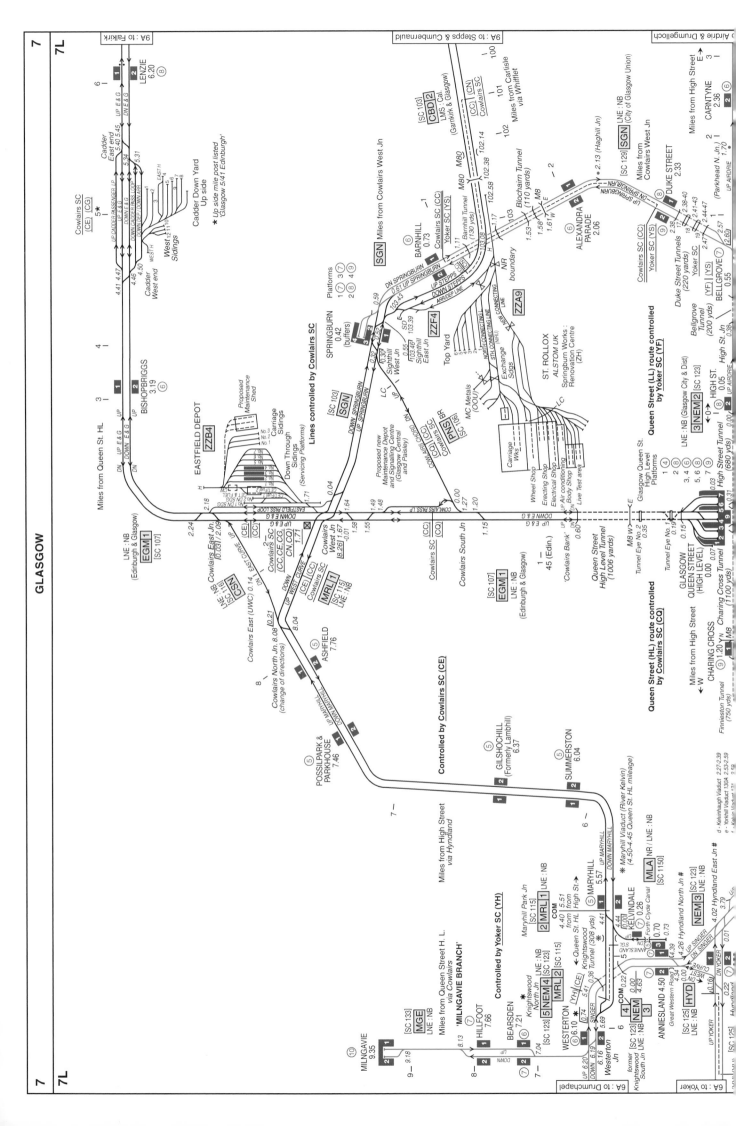

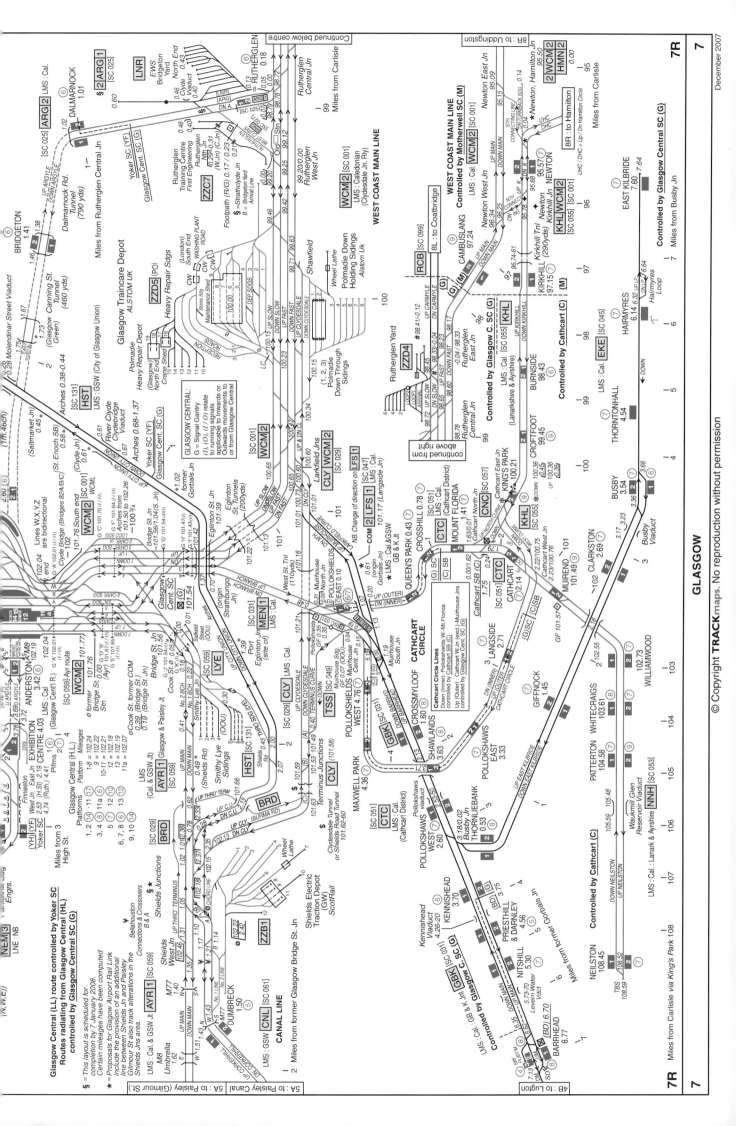

GLASGOW

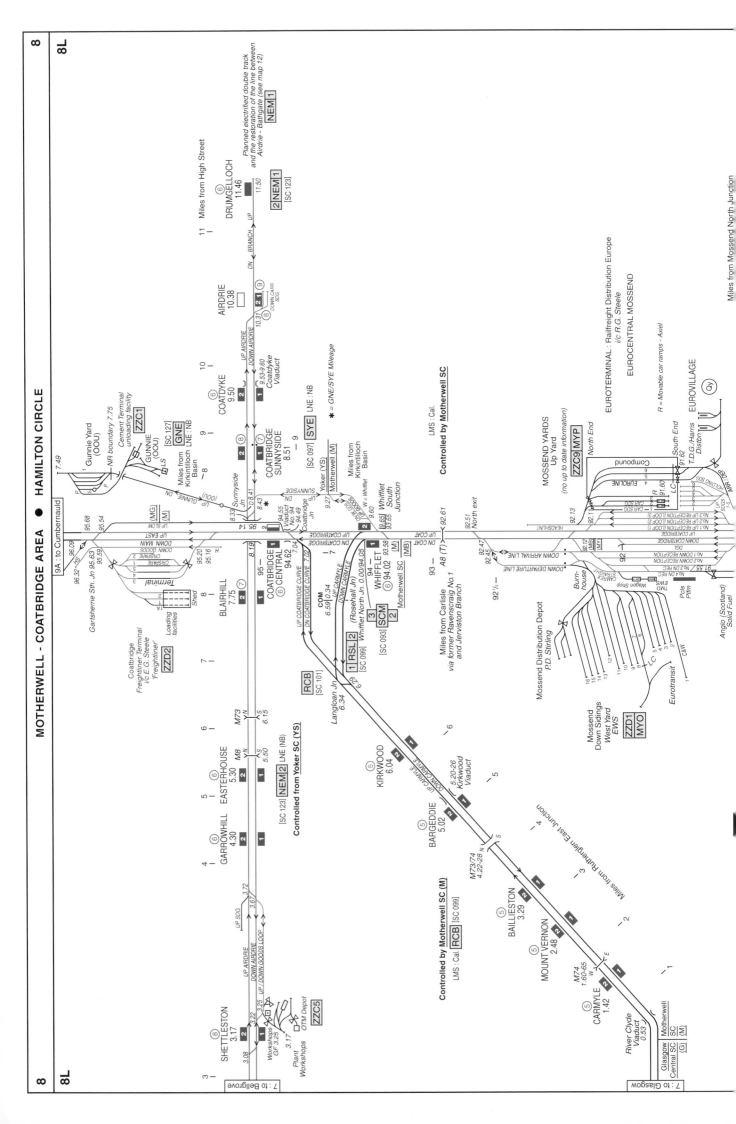

MOTHERWELL - COATBRIDGE AREA ● HAMILTON CIRCLE

8 8L

MOTHERWELL - COATBRIDGE AREA ● HAMILTON CIRCLE

© Copyright TRACKmaps. No reproduction without permission

December 2007

10D : to Fauld

SHOTTS 8.30 [1]

HARTWOOD 6.62 [1] [6]

[SC 007] [WWD] LMS : Cal. [EGS2] LMS : Cal.

Controlled by Motherwell SC

UP SHOTTS
DOWN SHOTTS

CARFIN 1.69 [1] [5]

CLELAND 3.52 [1] [6]

3.68-3.74 Cleland Viaduct

Calder (or Carfin) Viaduct 88.23-15

88.22

88.17

88 —

89 —

UP HOLYTOWN
DOWN HOLYTOWN

Miles from Carlisle

[SC 011] [WWD] LMS : Cal.

Controlled by Motherwell SC

Coltness Watsonhead Chapel Railhead

former Concrete Depot

RUN ROUND
ARR / DEP

NR bdy

COM 0.08
14.15

[1] [COS] 2

[SC 011] [WWD]

(Morning side) Up Sdgs

GF 83.40
83.41

15.19 UP BRANCH PL
UP PASS
DOWN MAIN

84.51

85 —

Wishaw Central Jn 86.57

[2] [1] WISHAW 86.31 [7]

86.63

86.71

Shieldmuir S. Jn 87.06

[SC 013] [SHR]

WISHAW CONNECTING LINE
87.43 LW
87.41 LM

87 —

87.26 Royal Mail Terminal

SHIELDMUIR 87.59 [6]

Corus : Dalzell Plate Works (General steel)

Former Wishaw & Coltness route via Ravenscraig to Jerviston Jn

87.70

88 —

88.19

88.44

88.63

Flemington 88.09

Slab bay

LC

Motherwell Signalling Centre (M, MB, MC, MG, MH, MS, MY)

88.77

[SC 001] [WCM2] LMS : Cal.

89 —

89.00
89.12

Lesmahagow Jn 89.51 / 89.50 (-0.01) SCM / HMN

Findlays GF 89.60

89.55

Motherwell Up Sdgs (or Findlays Sdgs)

MOTHERWELL 89.38 [13]

0.02

[13]

0.22

0.08 [12]

0.27

Engrs

UP BRAIDHURST GOODS LOOP
DOWN COATBRIDGE
UP COATBRIDGE

90.36

90.26

Braidhurst Viaduct (S. Calder Water)

90.17

90.25

Braidhurst No. 1 GF

LW

Bogies Shed

Wagon Repair Depot

North Sdgs

Former Motherwell Traction Maintenance Depot

90.00 (NIRU)

[ML] [ZZC8]

Back of Shops

Fitting Shop

ARR

Orbiston Viaduct No.24 (River Calder) 90.57-90.62 (Babylon Bridge)

Derby Sdgs (Car Sdgs)

Down Sdgs

Logans Road (LC) 89.77

06 —

Motherwell Weights Carriage Holding Sdgs [6] [2] [1]

AIRBLES 0.61

GL
ORC

UP HAMILTON
DN HAMILTON

0.0

89.59
89.53

[4]

[8]

= Haughhead Jns.

[SC 023] [HMN1]

COM (Ross Jn) 6.61 1.44 (Lesmahagow Jn)

from Newton, from Motherwell Hamilton Jn

6.37 [S] M74
[MH]

[M]

[2] [HMN2]

Camps Viaduct (River Clyde) 1.17 1.07

Allanton Loop

LARKHALL SINGLE

1.03

CHATELHERAULT 0.52 [6]

Barncluith Tunnel (360 yards)

Avon Water Viaduct

[MH]
[WH]
SD

Allanton Loop 0.63

[LRK] [SC 024] LMS : Cal. NR

MERRYTON 2.19 [6]

LARKHALL 2.78

2.64

[1] [2]

HAMILTON WEST 4.12 [8]

[9] [2] [1]

5.53
5.15
5.24

HAMILTON CENTRAL 5.03 [6]

Miles from Newton, Hamilton Jn

3.62
3.71

LOOP1
LP1

Wagon repair works
E.G. Steele

Crane

3.31 (Strathaven Jn)

UP HAMILTON CIRCLE
DOWN HAMILTON CIRCLE

3.56
3.46

TENNANTS HEADSHUNT

Earnock Sidings

OOU

former Tennants Loading bank (OOU)

BLANTYRE 2.29 [8]

[SC 023] [HMN2] LMS : Cal.

UP MAIN
DOWN MAIN

91 —

92 —

93 —

94 —

95 —

UDDINGSTON 93.71 [1] [7]

93.59
93.50 Uddingston Jn
93.29
94.16

M74

NEWTON 95.57

Newton, Hamilton Jn 95.50 0.00 WCM2 / HMN2

DN [2] [1]

7A : to Glas

STH CONNECTING LINE
ON TURNBACK SDG 0.14
0.04

DOWN MAIN

95.19

WEST COAST MAIN LINE [SC 001] [WCM2] LMS : Cal.

Controlled by Motherwell SC

BELLSHILL 2.30 [1] [7]

LMS : Cal. [EGS1] [SC 011]

Controlled by Motherwell SC

DOWN HOLYTOWN

91.50 Mossend W. Jn

[MDW] [SC 019]

UP WEST CURVE
DN WEST CURVE
91.08

91.17 UP E. CURVE
91.26 DN E. CURVE
3.34

Miles from Carlisle to Mossend South Jn

[MS] [M]

91.08

Ravenscraig Sdg

COM 91.03 (Jerviston S. Jn)

91.12/0.00 Mossend S. Jns

[JVN] [SC 017]

TB

[SC 093] [SCM1] LMS : Cal. (Motherwell Deviation)

Controlled by Motherwell SC

3.58 (Fullwood Jn)
0.37
3.61
[1] [EGS] 2

[MDE] $ [1] [SC 011]
(Milnwood Jn)

$ = Mossend S. Jn to Mossend E. Jn formerly Milnwood Jn to Fullwood Jn

[2] [SCM] 1 [SC 093]

1.35
1.28
[89.49] $
1.23
3.60

3.66

8R

NIRU 8R

8

[SC 001] LMS : Cal. [2] [WCM] [1]

84 —

84.00 Law Jn
84.09 Law-Law GF
84.10 DOWN MAIN
84.18 DOWN SDGS
84.20

Law Sth GF 83.38
Law Sth GF (OOU) 83.33

84.64
84.59

85 —

UP MAIN Garriongill Jn

WISHAW SOUTH 86.50

[SC 001] LMS : Cal.

86 —

87 —

Shieldmuir S. Jn

RM = Royal Mail Line

Miles from Carlisle

8

8R

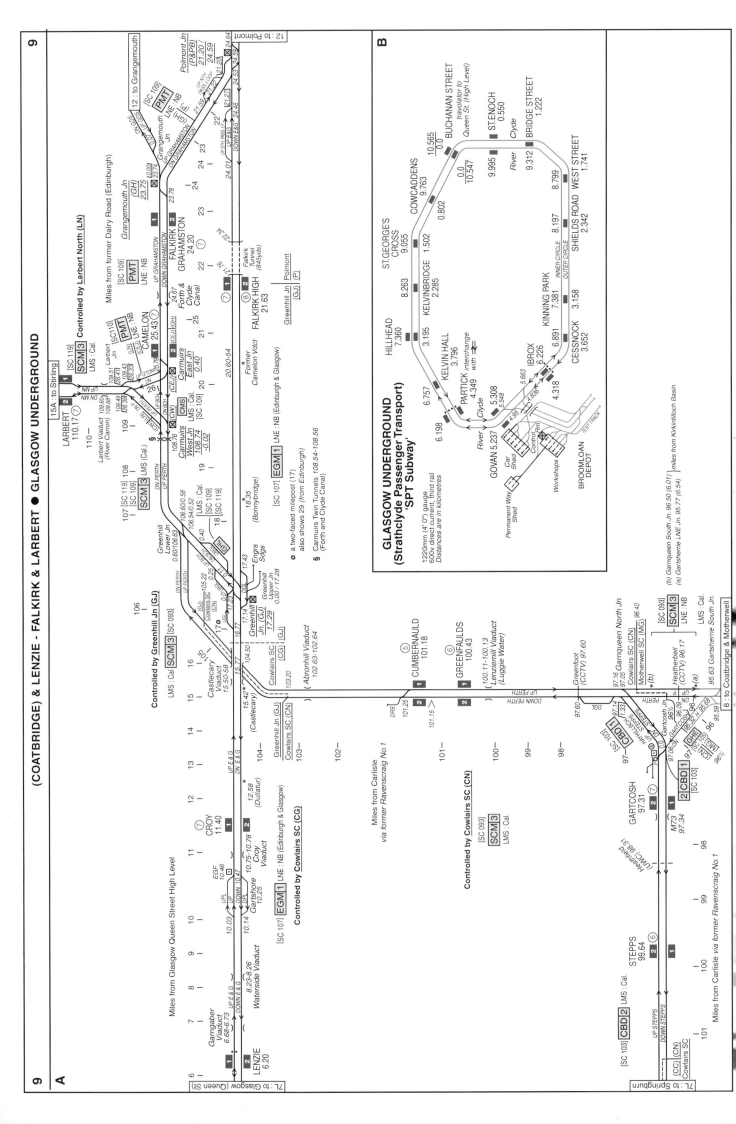

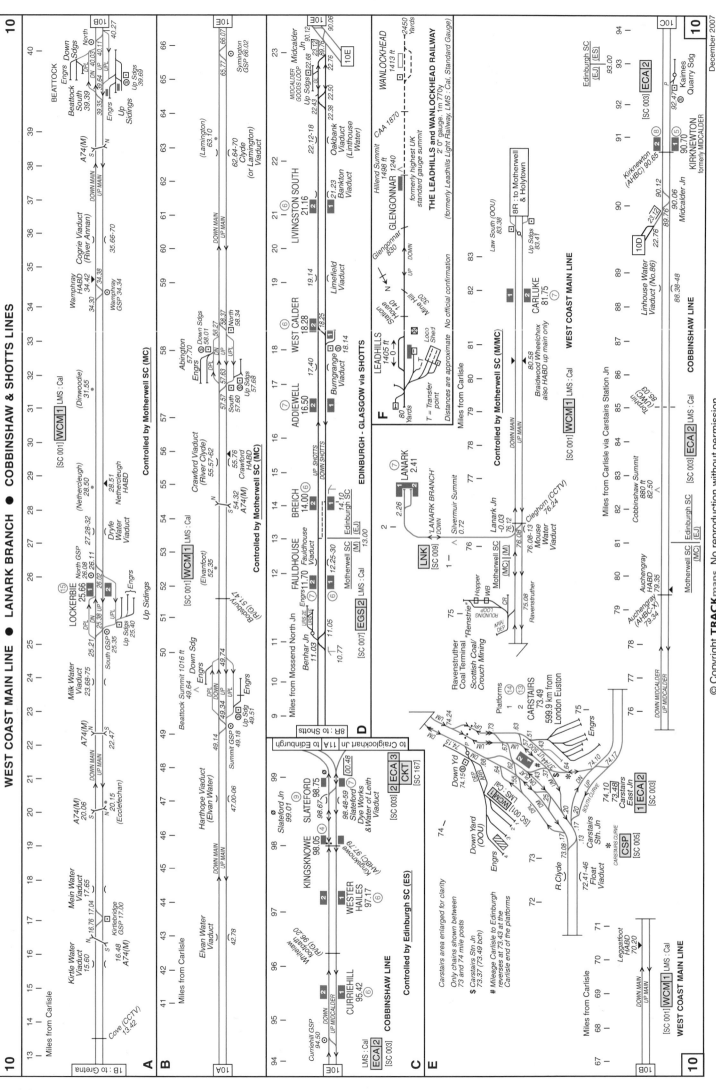

A

Edinburgh Waverley :
Platforms 12 to 18 are shown as electrified,
also lines 'X' and 'Y' through the Centre Mound Tunnel,
but this work is not expected to be
completed until February 2008

EDINBURGH WAVERLEY
Platforms

1	⑥	12	④
2	⑪	13	⑥
3	④	14	⑧
4	⑨	15	⑧
7	⑨	16	⑧
8	⑪	17	⑧
9	⑪	18	④
10	⑨	19	⑪
11	⑪	20	⑥

ZZB3

(a) [SC 147]
[SC 171]

Haymarket Depot (HA)
SCOTRAIL T&RS

Powderhall Compaction Plant
2.12   Mule   Edinb
1.76   District
1.78   NR Bdy   IN   1.54
OUT

West End   Shed
East End
EAST SDG 9
EAST SDG 8
EAST SDG 7
EAST SDG 6

(North)
45

Platforms
0   ⑨
1   ⑨
2-4 ⑪

LM = Light Maintenance
HEAVY MAINT. RD
LM 1
LM 2

1 (North)   ½

0

(632.793 Km from London, Kings Cross)
EDINBURGH WAVERLEY
Waverley Bridge
North ← 0.00 → South

[SC 153]
CPH
LNE : NB

(South) 46
Edinburgh SC
(EH) (E)

ECN 2   [SC 147]
[SC 171]
LNE : NB

20
19   2
17
16   3
15
14   4
13
12   11
7

ECN 2
W_8_E
W_6_E
W_4_E
W_2_E

FUEL RD

(W)

HAYMARKET
1.19

Haymarket
North Tunnel
(1040 yards)

Princes St.
Gardens   0.22
0.38   0.25   0.16
0.36   0.32   0.27

NORTH LOOP
NORTH
PLATF'M
10.04 X 0.07

0.27   Calton North
Tunnel (490 yds)
NORTH LINE   0.50

(631-5
Abbey
Jn
0.61

Haymarket
West Jn (a)
2.41

WEST
END H

UP
UP NORTH
DN NORTH

1.53 N GDS LP   1.40   TS
1.55   1.33
45.72

1   Mound
Tunnels
(130 yds)

Mri Sdgs
0.27
SOUTH PFM LOOP   0.110

½

Calton South
Tunnel
(400 yards)

(631-

2.28   44.76
44.79

44.73   44.75
GORGIE/
[SC 185]

Change of
direction

DN

10.111
Haymarket
Central Jn
UP   DN

2   3
4

UP SOUTH
DN SOUTH   1.30/45.71
100.41

Haymarket
South Tunnel
(1040 yards)
1.14

0.47

0.36   0.32   0.27
Y
X
W

U
UP SUBW
0.29
0.21   DOWN SUBURBAN

Waverley
East End
0.21/0.28

9 ECM 8
[SC 147]
LNE : NB

ECA 3
[SC003]
LMS : Cal

EGM 2
[SC 107]

EGM 2

SUB 2   [SC 169]

45.35

Miles from Carlisle 100

46.02   1.19
(Glas.)   (Edin.Wav.)

EGM 3
LNE : NB

9   8
DOWN SUBURBAN

Waverley
West End
0.15

☒
Edinburgh
Signalling
Centre (E) *
0.07

ECN 2
LNE : NB

[SC 107]

GGE

1 EGM 2

[SC 107]
LNE : NB

-0.03
0.48
0.00
0.45
Gorgie Jn

COM
(South Lines only)

2 EGM 3
[SC 107]

[SC 171]   2 ECN 1
[SC 107]   3 EGM 4
LNE : NB

Ω = At buffer stops of platforms 12 &13

*= E, EA, EB, EC, ED, EF, EG, EH,
EM, EN, EO, EP, ER, ES, ET, EU

[SC 003]
2 ECA 3
Slateford Jn
99.01
00.48

99.20

99.39

44.75

DOWN MIDCALDER
UP MIDCALDER
(ES)(EH)   99.60
Edinburgh SC

Ω I
0

[SC 147/171]   1 ECN ECM 9   [SC 147]
[SC 107]   4 EGM
LNE : NB

99.15
99.17 Engineers'
Jarvis

SUB 2   [SC 165]

Slateford Yard   ZZB9

Engrs
Plant
Shed

UP BRANCH
DOWN BRANCH

Craiglockhart Jn 0.00/1.17
Craiglockhart Tunnel (60 yds)
1.18
1.20

Miles from Haymarket Central Jn

2   3   4

CRAIGLOCKHART LOOP

CKT   [SC 167]

CRAIGLOCKHART
1.23

Controlled by Edinburgh SC (ES)

★ = Scotrail Carriage Sidings
❖ = West Sidings

MORNINGSIDE ROAD
2.06

UP (INNER) SUBURBAN
DOWN (OUTER) SUBURBAN

Newington
3.50

Edinburgh SC
(ES) (EP)
4.00

2.60
(Blackford Hill)

B

All lines controlled by Edinburgh SC

19   20   21   22
[SC 149]   NBK   LNE : NB
NORTH BERWICK
22.25

Miles from Edinburgh Waverley

11   12   13   14   15   16   17   18

[SC 147]   ECM 8   LNE : NB (Edinburgh and Berwick)

St. Germains
(CCTV)
11.52 (614-000)

EAST COAST MAIN LINE

Engrs
Up
GF
17.50   1
UPL

Drem Jn
18.15
18.15

NORTH
BERWICK   UP
22.22

19   20   21   22   23
[SC 147]   ECM 8   LNE : NB (Edinburgh and Berwick)

24   25   26

Stenton
HABD
25.48

10.31
D

1
17.66   17.79
DN BERWICK

18.21
DPL

UP BERWICK
DOWN BERWICK

24.38   24.49

Bunker

Former Blindwells Extension
Opencast Disposal Point

LONGNIDDRY
13.18 (611.431)
(EA) (EF)
⑥   Edinburgh SC
14.20

DREM
17.60
(604.173)
⑦   2

20.60
(East Fortune)

Markle (AHBC)
22.14 (597-035)

(EF) (ED)
Edinburgh SC
23.60

24.42
Stenton
GSP

Knowes (UWC)
24.57

C

Miles from Edinburgh Waverley

32   33   34   35   36   37   38   39   40   41   42   43   44

Dunbar Rail Terminal
Viridor Waste Haul

Torness Power Station
British Energy
GSP

Innerwick
Wheelchex
33.62

Controlled by Edinburgh SC

(Cockburnspath)
36.42
(573.997)

Penmanshiel
Tunnel diversion
(1979)
39½ 40

Grantshouse
41.08
(566.405)
Up Sdgs
Engrs

EAST COAST
MAIN LINE

Pad
31.07

32.77

34.28   34.40

UPL
41.13

31.13   31.21
SMALL LOOP

32.65
Oxwellmains
HABD

Innerwick
34.34

Dunglas Viaduct
36.02-08

(old tunnel
39.52-64)   40.20

40.47
40.20

DPL
400 ft

ARR/DEP   No. 1 Sdg
No. 2
No. 3
FP

Loading
point   LARGE LOOP
(31.20)   Vehicle
Maintenance Shed

(ED) (EG)
Edinburgh SC
33.60

Oxwellmains (Down) Cement Works
Lafarge

Kilometre posts are on the down side : distances from London (Kings Cross), in round brackets

Albert Dock
Lafarge LC
Grain terminal
Edinburgh Dock
Coal Hopper
General American Transport (STS)
Firth of Forth
LEITH DOCKS
Forth Ports Authority

Storage Services (Leith) Ltd (STS)
2 I.M.Cowe
3 Storage Services
4 GRAND DISCHARGE LONG LYE
5 ROUNDING RD
6 ROUNDING RD
SHED RD
COAL RD
BACK RD
THIRD LINE
DOCK LINE
MSGR LINE

LC open
Forth Ports Gate
NR Bdy
Marine Road LC (open)
EWS Gate
Car ramp
SPUR

LEITH SOUTH

Depot and Dock areas subject to track layout changes

Pipe Roads
— 2½

LEITH SOUTH YARD

1 DYKE
2 RECEPTION RD

2.20
2.16 Seafield (TMO)

Cockenzie Power Station
Scottish Power
Unloading shed
CR

LNE : NB
LHS 1 Controlled by Edinburgh SC (EP)
[SC 151]
— 2

WDERHALL BRANCH

8.27 Slued to west 2003 9.39

1
2 former MEADOWBANK STADIUM
Powderhall Branch Jn .70

0.50 Baileyfield Switch and Crossing Wks
0.61 (VAE)
Baileyfield
0.33
0.17 Portobello Sdgs (NIRU)
Crane
Portobello Jns
OHLE Stabling Sdg
JOPPA STRAIGHT
0.07 (A)
0.04
Joppa

[SC 147] ECM 8 LNE : NB (Edinburgh and Berwick)
4   5   6   (Inveresk)   7   8   9   10
MUSSELBURGH 6
5.00-5.13 (624.464)
1
Monktonhall Jn 6.40
5.78 (Edinburgh)
WALLYFORD 7
7.54
1
Engrs
Up Sdgs
UPL 9.72
6 1

UP BERWICK
DOWN BERWICK

2.16
No.1 REC/DEP CW WASHER RD
No.2 REC/DEP
M3 DEP
No.4 DEP
TANK RD
H1 H2 H3
19
20 21
entinny
EB
FR
M
CC
2.75
3.25 3.30 3.47
3.36 (C)
3.37 (D)
Repair Shed Sdg
Wheel Lathe Sdg Shed
underfloor wheel lathe
Maintenance Depot
UP DOWN
DN UP

UP BERWICK
DOWN BERWICK
9.42
9.64 10.04
ECM 8
[SC 147]
LNE : NB

Edinburgh SC (EM) 2 5.66
Edinburgh SC (EM)
Millerhill (M)
1
MHL
2
[SC 155]
Wanton Walls 5.60 COM
1.40
'Sorts Sdgs' 1-10
ME Sdgs
Engrs

6.11 (Millerhill)
8.20
(EM) (EA)
Edinburgh SC
PRESTONPANS 9
9.40 (617.500)

§ DN DN
§
MLE [SC 157]
*

Craigentinny Depot
National Express East Coast
2.40 (EC)

B = BY-PASS ROAD
R = Repair Shed
I = Inspection Shed
M = Maintenance Shed
CC = Carriage Cleaning Shed

former Niddrie North Junction
1
SUB COM
2
[SC 163]
LNE : NB

BRUNSTANE
3.72
— 4
[SC 161]
NDE 1
LNE : NB

Edinburgh SC (EP)
Millerhill (M)
Millerhill (M)
Niddrie South Jn
5.02

DOWN GOODS
UP GOODS

1
OTP 2
[SC 155]
MHL 3
Millerhill West Jn
Used Ballast Stockpile
Coal Loading Sdg
Reclamation Depot
Millerhill Yard
5.50
Engrs

Millerhill Loco Fuelling Point
BACK/DEP (b)
MID
SHED
FUEL
CHUTE
ARR

5.53
5.55
5.51
to former Monktonhall Colliery

Millerhill East Jn Jn
0.29/0.0
(a)
Millerhill South Jn
1 NDE 2 [SC 159]
§ *
5.64 3.72
W. CURVE
SOUTH CURVE
NO.6 ENGINE RELEASE
OOU former Elect. Depot OOU
LC
4
3
2
1
6.04
former Waverley Route to Carlisle (page 1A)

(a) M.c. origin at Millerhill S Jn and runs to Wanton Walls

6.47
6.52

5
UDDINGSTON
5.07

6
LNE : NB SUB 2 [SC 165]

EDINBURGH SUBURBAN
6.30

5.20
(St. Leonards Jn)

Niddrie West Jn
NIDDRIE CURVE (BRANCH)
7.08
4.54
NEWCRAIGHALL 7
5
MHY
[SC 165]
(Millerhill Yard Lines)

4.46
4.64 DN MAIN
4.70
TB 5.02
5.10
UP MAIN
DOWN
5.21

Millerhill Yard Jn
NDE 1 [SC161]

Millerhill Yard Sdgs (EWS)
A - Alec
B - Bobby
C - Charlie
D - Davie
E - Eddie
F - Freddy

Alternative Designations:
SDG F4 - No. 1 Reception
SDG F5 - No. 1 Reception
SDG F6 - Up Millerhill
SDG F7 - Down Millerhill

(b) = Ballast loading sdgs
= D6 'Royal Scotsman maintenance sdg

29   30   31
DUNBAR
29.05
(585.950) 12
Engrs
DN & UP PL
28.66
29.10 Up Sdgs GF
29.22
11C
28.31 Dunbar West
29.03 Down Sdgs GF
Engrs
29.49 Dunbar East
OHC

47   48   49   50   51   52   53   54
[SC 147] ECM 8 LNE : NB (Edinburgh and Berwick)
(Edinburgh and Berwick) LNE : NB
LNE : NE (Newcastle and Berwick)

Up Sdg
46.22
Reston GSP
47.14
47.11 / 47.20
Engrs
Down Sdg

(Burnmouth)
51.60
Lamberton
53.71
(544.751)
former regional boundary
COM
Lamberton HABD
69.60

BERWICK-UPON-TWEED
67.00 (540.189)
11
67.38 UGL
66.74 66.41
Viaduct
UP MAIN
DN MAIN

UP BERWICK
DOWN BERWICK
50.20
(Ayton)
54.50 69.67
Edinburgh SC (EG) Tweedmouth (TW)
SC LNE
[SC 147] 8 ECM 7 [LN 600]
69   68   Miles from Newcastle

68.01/56.35
former Marshall Meadows
67.36
67.08
2 1
Royal Border Bridge
Down North Sdgs
66.33-30
Tweedmouth (TW) 65.78
66
67
2 : 23B to Newcastle

EDINBURGH AREA ● EAST COAST MAIN LINE TO BERWICK

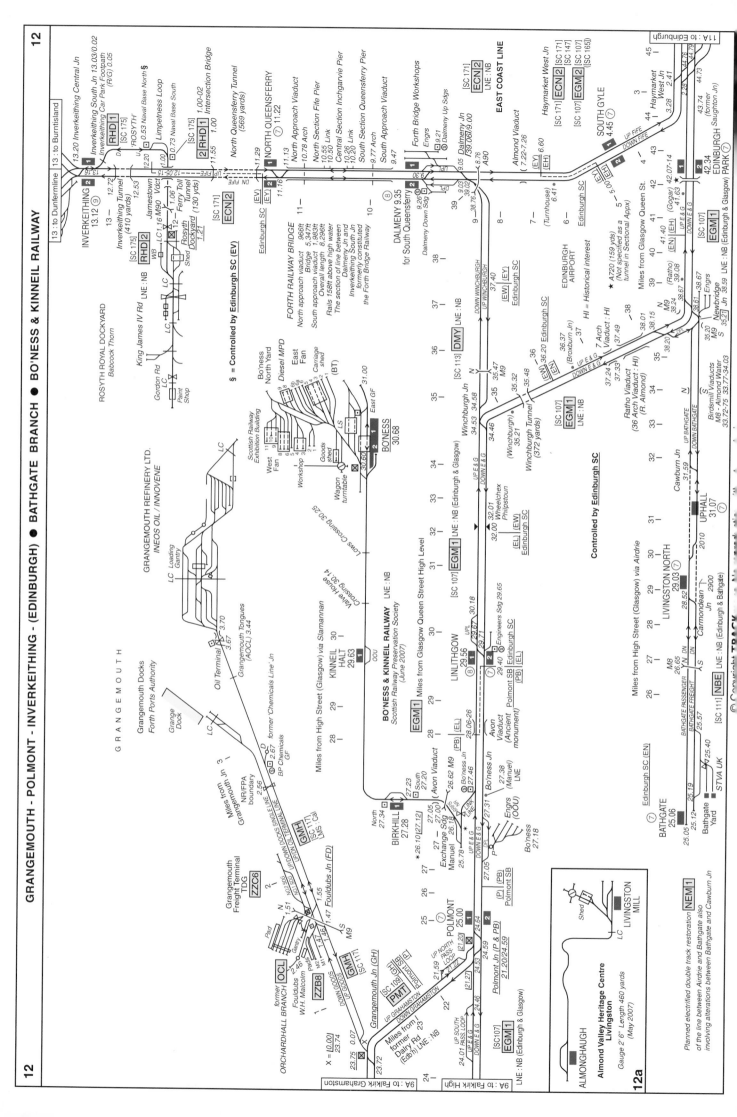

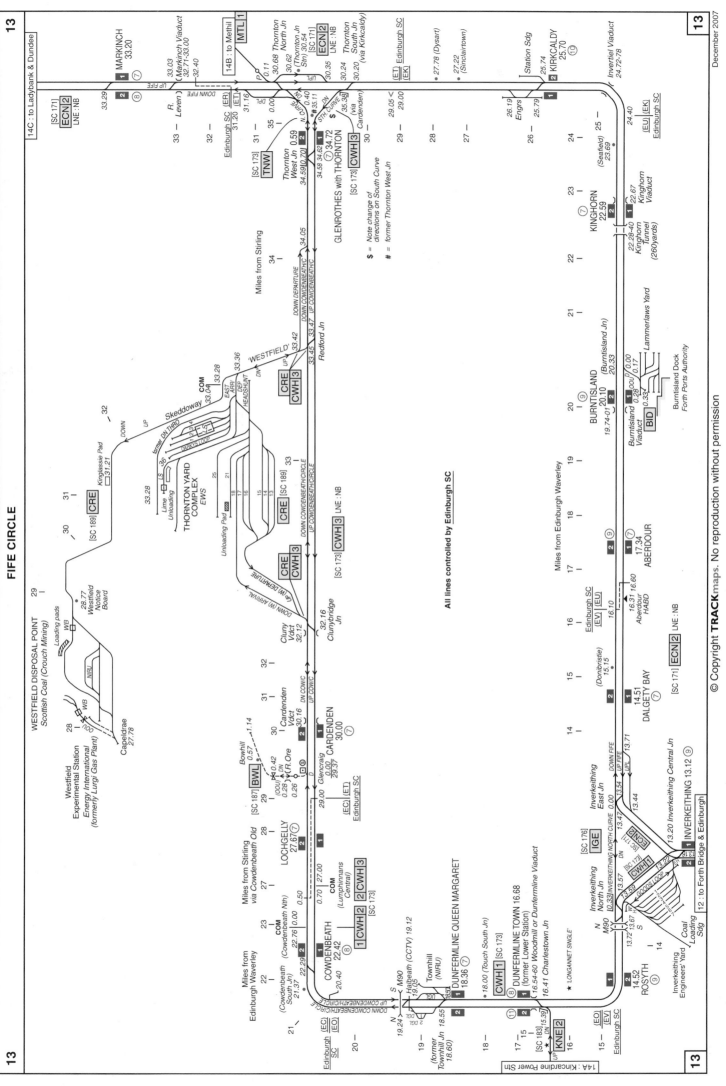

FIFE CIRCLE

December 2007

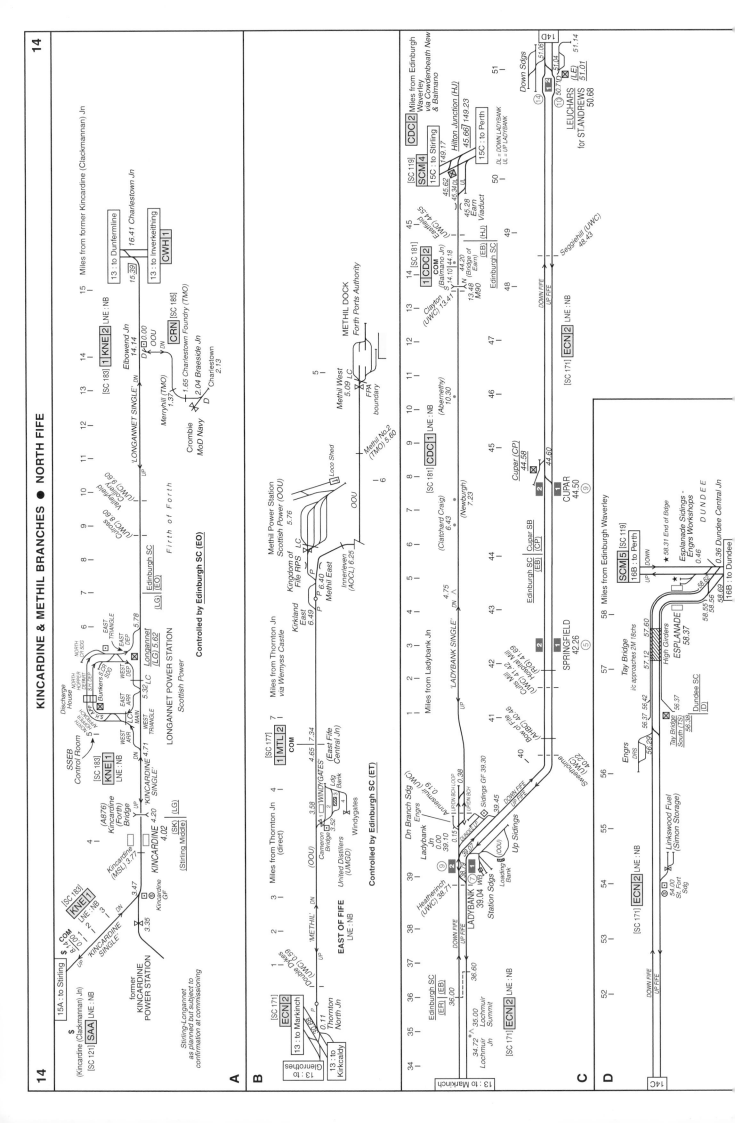

LARBERT - STIRLING - PERTH

Miles from Carlisle via former Ravenscraig No.1

Column A (top)

Platforms ⑦ ⑧ ⑧

DUNBLANE 123.19
Engrs 123.34
123.47-50 Allanwater Viaduct
Kippenross Tnl (610 yards) (Historical Interest)
122.73 Kippenross Vdct
122.66 SG 123.10 (DB) (Oban Jn)
3 SCM 4 [SC 119]
123.40 (Oban Jn) 123.29

122.38 122.52 (SN) 121.39 (SN) Down IBS
122.34 Mill o'Keir Viaduct

BRIDGE OF ALLAN 121.10 ⑦
Bridge of Allan Down IBS 121.10
120.66 Bridge of Allan Up IBS (DB)
2   1
Cornton (AHBC) (SN) 120.10
Cornton No.2 FP
Cornton (R/G) 119.60
120.22-24 Cornton Viaduct

Causewayhead Jn 119
1.05
'KINCARDINE SINGLE' DN
Waterside (CCTV) 1.46 UP

118.61 118.68
Forth Viaducts 0.66
0.58
DN KINCARDINE 0.58
UP KINCARDINE
(formerly Down & Up S&D Lines)

Stirling - Longannet: As planned but subject to confirmation at commissioning

[SC 121] SAA   LNE : NB

LNE : NB
[SC 121] SAA KNE 1
[SC 183] LNE : NB

(Kincardine (Clackmannan) Jn)
8.14 (Clackmannan Jn) 0.00
* COM 0.00

Column A (lower, Stirling detail)

STIRLING 118.24
0.15
Stirling North (SN) 118.38/0.29
118.47 118.44
118.38
Centre Sdgs
2   3   4,5   6
8,6   9 10
Kincardine Lines
UP MAIN / DN MAIN
UP SDG / UP SDG2
UP SPUR
Stirling Middle (SM/SK)
118.08/-0.01
ZZD5
117.76 118.03
[SC 119] SCM 3
(SM) (SK)
[SC 121] SAA
(Clay Slags (UWC) 117.21)

Platforms
② ⑮ ⑧ ⑤
③ ⑮ ⑥ ⑪
⑨ ⑩ ⑬

Polmaise Down IBS 116.64
116.37 Polmaise Up IBS
116.00 (Bannockburn)

Controlled by Stirling Middle (SK)

Miles from Stirling Middle

A91 2.36 — 2
— 3
— 4
Manor Neuk (UWC) 2.59
Manor Powis (UWC) 2.71
Blackgrange (CCTV) 3.47

(Cambus Jn) 4.39
(Cambus) 4.55 *
Cambus (CCTV) 4.59
4.67 Cambus West Jn
5.38 Cambus East Jn
'KINCARDINE' 5 DN / 6 UP
Alloa Stn 6.67 Jn   a   b
CAMBUS LOOP
ALLOA 6.77
'KINCARDINE' 7
ALLOA LOOP
* COM 8.14 0.00

14A : to Dunfermline

a = Alloa West Jn 7.36
b = Alloa East Jn 8.05

PERTH (NEW) YARD area (top right)

19A : to Dunkeld & Birnam
153

PERTH (NEW) YARD 152.68
Plant Depot : Jarvis
Muirhead : EWS (PH)
NDT Shed
Wagon Shops
Load 9 Bank
Engrs / Ballast / Loading
Depot
COAL RD / MID ROAD
ENGINE ROAD
FRONT LOOP
DOWN SDGS
UP SDGS
Turntable
Muirton 152.32
(SJ) Stanley Jn 152.54
(P) 152.54
[SC 193] HGL 1   LMS : Cal (Scottish Midland)

Column B

Miles from Carlisle via former Ravenscraig No.1

15B 118

GLENEAGLES 135.50
135.10
⑩ ② ①
137 136 135 134 133

15C

Blackford (BK) 133.28
(MCB) 133.20
Engrs 133.18 DRS
URS
Machine Sdg
Loading banks

Boreland Farm (UWC) 132.20
Carsebreck No.1 (UWC) 131.07

Auchterarder 137.44
(AR) 137.41
137.31 DRS
137.17-24 Engrs URS
132 131 130 129 128 127 126 125

Drumallan (UWC) 126.27
Quoigs No.1 (UWC) 128.01

Greenloaning (GL) 129.17
129.28 DN
129.06 UP UGL
DGL

Barbush Viaduct 124.15

[SC 119] SCM 4   LMS : Cal (Scottish Central)

A   15A

Column C / D (Perth area)

15C 15D

Hilton Jn (HJ) 149.23
M90
Kirkton or Mailer No.2 (UWC) 148.66
Moncrieffe Tunnel (1210 yards) 150.04
45.66 M90
149.29 45.34
149.17/45.62 DN
14C : to Ladybank
DL = DOWN LADYBANK
UL = UP LADYBANK
CDC 2 [SC 181]

Earn Viaduct 147.55.65
Forgandenny Ford (UWC) (HJ) 147.39
Broombarns (UWC) (HJ) 146.31
Fortevict Farm (UWC) (HJ) 145.13
Fortevict (AHBC-X) (HJ) 144.45
River May Viaduct 144.50-53

Baldinnies No.1 (UWC) (HJ) 142.70
Easter Balgour (UWC) (HJ) 142.96
Broadslap (UWC) (HJ) 141.02
Whitemoss (AHBC-X) (HJ) 140.24

150 149 148 147 146 145 144 143 142 141 140 139 138

[SC 119] SCM 4   LMS : Cal (Scottish Central)

B   15A

Column D (Perth)

Miles from Carlisle via former Ravenscraig No.1

(Joint Stn : Cal : NB : High)
⊘ 151.36 is zero for HGL2 mileage to Inverness

PERTH (P) 151.05 / 151.25
151.41 / 151.48
Dovecoteland 151.42
Earls Dykes
Holding Sdgs (OOU)
Up Carriage Sdgs 151.34
'SCOTRAIL'
(Alt 32ft)
S 6 7 N
S 5 4 N
Platforms
1 ⑪ 5 ⑩ 8
2 ⑨ 6 ⑥ ②
3 ⑥ 7 ②
4 ②

150.79 151.04 DN F 151.12
Perth South Jn 150.60
150.57 150.61
150.59 151.09 DN DUNDEE 151.04
UP DUNDEE
UP DUNDEE LOOP
DN DUNDEE LOOP
Carriage Sdgs
McPherson's Sdg (OOU)
St.Leonards Jn
COM Dundee Lines
(a) 151.03 (b) 151.08
21.01 20.76
Orchardbank 20.51
20.64
Miles from Dundee

16A : to Dundee

[SC 119] 4 SCM HGL 1 [SC 193]
SCM 5 [SC 119]

Miles from Carlisle via former Ravenscraig No.1

150.04 M90
Moncrieffe Tunnel (1210 yards)
DRS S N
DOWN MAIN / UP MAIN
150 151 152 153

LMS : Cal (Scottish Central)

C   15C   15

December 2007

Column A (far left, Larbert)

Larbert-Stirling: Rationalisation Proposals -
Closure of Plean Jn SB and restoration of UGL at Larbert

LARBERT 110.17 ⑦
Larbert North (LN) 110.30
110.32 110.27
110.58 110.22
Engrs former Ballast Loading Dock (OOU)
DN/DS YRD
DN M / UP M
UGL
D
1   2

Larbert North H
M876 111.11
M9 111.22
112.52
112.31 (Alloa Jn)
N S
Plean Jn (PJ) 114.26
M9

DOWN MAIN / UP MAIN

[SC 119] SCM 3   LMS : Cal (Scottish Central)

9A : to Carmuirs Jns

111 112 113 114 115 116 117 118

D   15A

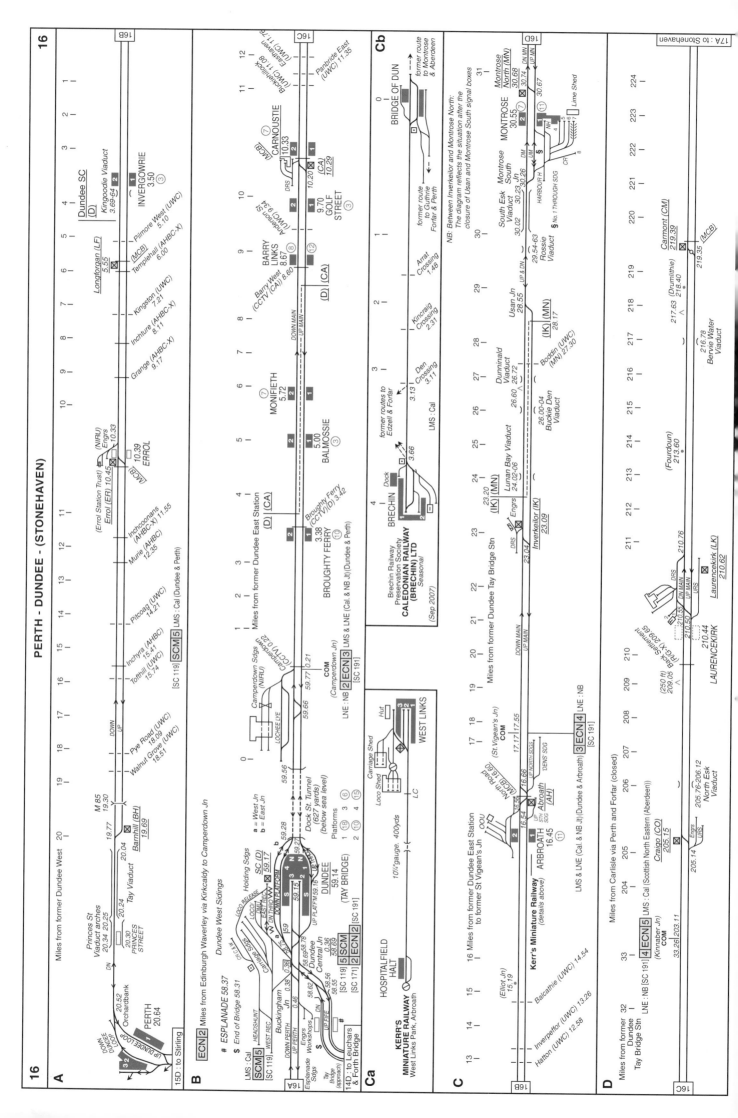

PERTH - DUNDEE - (STONEHAVEN)

STONEHAVEN - ABERDEEN - KEITH - DUFFTOWN ● ALFORD VALLEY RAILWAY

A

Miles from Carlisle via Perth & Forfar (Closed)

16D : to Montrose

241 0

[SC191] [ECN|5] LMS : Cal (Scottish North Eastern (Aberdeen))

[SC191] [SC195]
5 [ECN] [ANI]1
COM 241.08/0.00
N
FUEL
S 7
S 5 4
3
ABERDEEN (Jt. Stn)
241.06
240.73
17B
240.15
240.63

National Express East Coast
Aberdeen (A)
Aberdeen Clayhills Depot (AC)
240.62
HST CW
FERRYHILL
FERRYHILL UP/DN
240.65
DN MAIN
UP MAIN
240.40
240.37
Ferryhill Jn
GDS
Dykes Side
Fuel Point
LHS
LHS 2
LHS 3
10 o'CLOCK STUMP

Ferryhill Down Sidings

GUD

ABERDEEN Guild Street
(Closure Envisaged)

British Fuels Aberdeen Coal (J.G. Russell)
CALEY BANK
SHORE RD
SHORE RD BR.
10 o'CLOCK BR.
0.24
0.16
0.00
RUSSELL'S BR.
Crane
Craiginches Yard Down Sdgs

R. Dee
R. Dee Vdct
240.03

Craiginches North Sdgs
240.08-22

DOWN MAIN
UP MAIN
LOOP 1
LOOP 2
239.32
239.27
Up Yard
S-H
239.50
Lafarge
BC1
BC2
SS1
SS2
Craiginches South
239.30

Ci = Craiginches North 239.77
J = Aberdeen South Jn 240.76/0.37

ABERDEEN Platforms

3	⑪
4	⑪
5	⑫
6	12&10 (25)
7	9&9 (21)

Bb

ROYAL DEESIDE RAILWAY PRESERVATION SOCIETY

14½
Banchory
2¾ mile
MILTON OF CRATHES
¼ mile standard guage (Aug 2007)

Ba

ALFORD VALLEY RAILWAY CO. LTD.
Old Station, Alford
2'0" (610mm) gauge
3km
(June 2007)

HAUGHTON PARK
KEMNAY BURN
ALFORD
Loco Shed

225 0

Miles from Aberdeen

⑨ STONEHAVEN
2
224.74
(SV)
224.64
224.75
224.22-33
Fetteresso Viaduct
DRS
URS
8
UP Shunting Sdgs (NIRU)
225.02
225.32
Glenury Viaduct
225.47
Cowie Den)
226.77-227.03
Den of Cowie Viaduct (344)
Muchalls Mill Viaduct
229.03-08½
227½
227

B

Miles from Aberdeen

Controlled by
Aberdeen (A) | Dyce Jn (DY)

[SC197]
WRO
LNE : GN of S

Hutcheon St KITTYBREWSTER
1.30
1.59
1.53
1.31
Kittybrewster
Schoolhill Tunnel (250 yards)
Hutcheon St Tunnel (280 yds)
0.75
0.67
0.54
0.43
0.32
0.17
0.15/0.17
0.03
ABERDEEN NORTH SDG
Dykeside
Gantry
Stump
ABERDEEN WATERLOO
Omya UK
0.08½

[SC195] [ANI]1 LNE : GN of S

PORTLETHEN 232.70
⑥
2
1

Cove Bay
236.20

Cairnrobin (UWC) 234.64

Newtonhill (NH) 230.60
DRS
URS
230.66
Elsick Viaduct
231.03-10

Muchalls Viaduct
229.65-70½

17A

17B

C

17B
Port Elphinstone
River Don Viaduct
15.59
15.16
LOOP 1 H
LOOP 2 H
TRTS 1
TRTS 2
Federal Tait
16.56
16.72
INVERURIE
16.79 (IE)
17.10
OOU
Engrs/Ballast
Down Sdgs
Lime
Timber
8
8
1
2
9

15.16

15

Miles from Aberdeen

16 17

'SINGLE' DN
UP

KINALDIE 10.43
'SINGLE' DN

Kirkton of Kinellar (UWC) 11.29
Boat of Kintore (AHBC) 12.78
13.29
Cairnhall (UWC) 14.22
Fullerton (UWC) 14.46

15
(KINTORE)

17C

Raith's Farm Freight Terminal
4
3
2
1
Wash area
Raith's Farm RF
NORTH ARDBEP LINE
GROUNDING LINE 6.67
SOUTH ARRV
DEP LINE
6.40
6.61
7.04
7.12
Wash area controlled by Shunter's Panel RF

DYCE 6.20
⑧
1
2
6.03
Dyce (DY) 6.11

BUCKSBURN 4.04
Buckaburn Viaduct
4.07
'SINGLE' DN

Pittodrie (RLC)
8.20

D

17D

Kennethmont Stn (UWC) 32.61
Down Sdgs
33.04
(Keith Hall) (UWC) 33.33
OOU
URS
32.15
Kennethmont (KN)
32.71

33 32 31 30

DOWN
UP

Shevock (UWC)
28.65

(Dunnideer)

INSCH 27.42
[MCB]
2 (IH)
1
27.47
27.39
27.31
Engrs/ DRS
⑥

Oyne (AHBC) 24.51
Pitcaple) 21.29
Buchanstone (UWC) 25.57
Lennington Farm (UWC) 25.37
Durno (UWC) 26.55

17E
* Goods Sdgs
Macphersons Transp't
53.26
DFN [SC199]
KEITH
30.23 ⑨
53.19
30.34
Keith (KJ) 30.35
53.05 30.40
COM
53.05/30.40
Miles from Forres 30

* *
New Sdgs
Chivas Distillery (OOU)
LOOP
DN SDG
MAIN
30.40
52.48

[SC195] [ANI]2 LMS : High. (Inverness & Aberdeen Jn Rly)

[SC195] [ANI]1 LNE : GN of S

Inverness & Aberdeen Jn

LMS : GN of S [SC195] [1] [ANI]2
[SC195] [ANI]1 LMS : High. (Inverness & Aberdeen Jn Rly)

Spey Viaduct 22.65

Deanshillock (UWC) 19.69
(Orbiston)

18A : to Elgin

19 20 21 22 23 24 25 26

MULBEN 25.30

DOWN

(Orbiston)
Rosarie (AOCR) 27.20
Tarn (UWC) 25.16
Bridgend (UWC) 28.22
Mortlach (UWC) 28.20
Midearnie No.1 (UWC) 27.29
Midearnie No.2 (UWC) 28.20
Bush (UWC) 27.29

Miles from Forres

F
17D

E

[SC199] DFN LNE : GN of S

Miles from Aberdeen

KEITH TOWN 53.66
53.36
53.50
NR K & DRA
K & DRA
53.26
(May 2007)

54 55 56 57 58 59 60 61 62 63 64

Strathmill Distillery
54.17
Earlyfolds (AHBC) 34.74
Toll of Cliffs (UWC) 34.52
Candy Farm (UWC) 34.40
Greenbank (UWC) 35.67
Towiemore 57.67
AUCHINDACHY (Private) 56.54
56.54

KEITH AND DUFFTOWN RAILWAY ASSOCIATION

DRUMMUIR 59.46

Viaduct No. 227 63.34-37
River Fiddich 63.61 63.77
DUFFTOWN 64.00
64.08

[SC195] [ANI]1 LNE : GN of S

HUNTLY 40.67
(HT) 40.43
40.42
LP
MN
⑨
8
1
2
9
40.78
Up Sdgs NIRU
Goods Sdgs

[SC195] [ANI]1 LNE : GN of S

Deveron (Rothiemay) Viaduct 45.05
45.24 (Rothiemay)

Little Mill (UWC) 46.41
Burnmouth (UWC) 49.62
48.79 (Grange Jn)

17C

17D

17

© Copyright **TRACK**maps. No reproduction without permission

December 2007

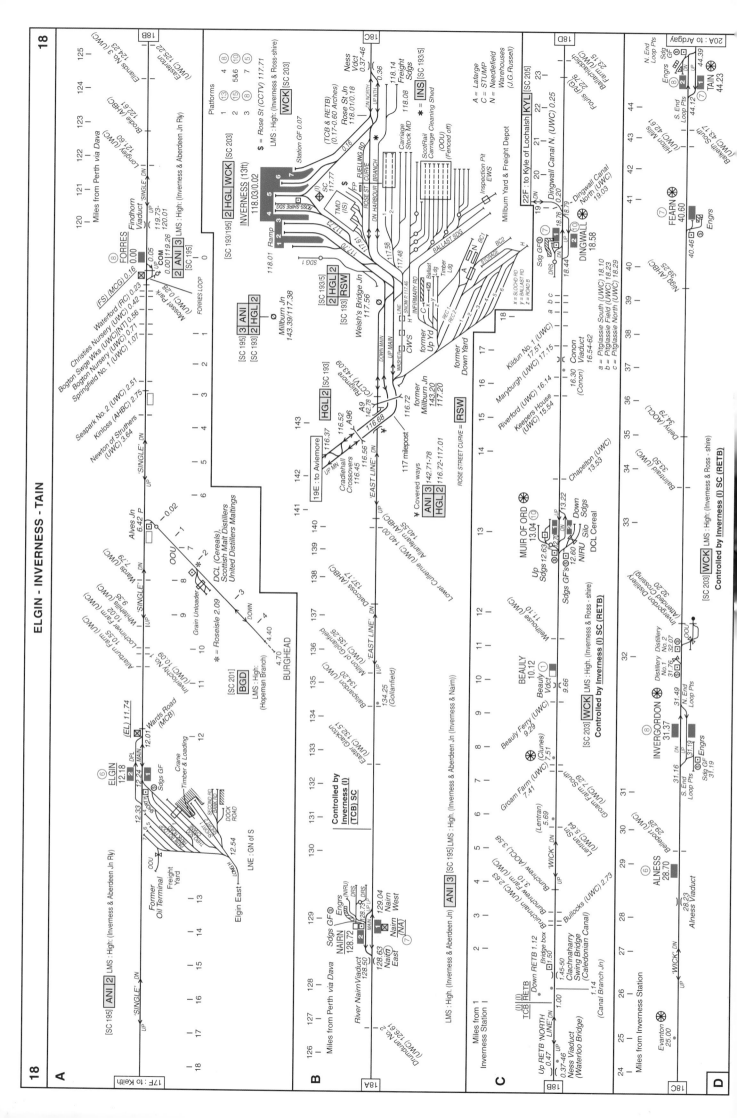

Row A

Miles from Carlisle via former Ravenscraig No.1

Miles from Perth (former Highland platform 151.36)

154 155 156 157 158 8 9 10 11 12 13 14 15 16 17 18 19 20 21 22 23 24 25 26 27 28

LMS : Cal. (Scottish North Eastern (Scottish Midland))

Schochie   Ordie
Viaduct   Viaduct
156.00   156.18

155.38
(Luncarty)

Charleson   Kinclaven
(UWC) 8.32   (DWJ) 8.63

Murthly (AHBC)
10.15

Easter
Dalguise
(UWC)'s
20.02

Inchmagranachan
(UWC)'s
No.2 18.36
No.3 18.57

Inver
Viaduct
16.50

16.55-72
Inver Tunnel
(350 yds)

20.48
River Tay
Viaduct

Dalguise
No.1 19.76

Guay (UWC)
21.29

Haugh of Tullymet
(UWC) 22.67

(Ballinluig)
23.40

Moulinearn (R/G)
25.33

Pitlochry

1 HGL 2 [SC 193]

Stanley Jn (SJ)
7.07

158.35
158.38 7.02
COM

'SINGLE' DN

DOWN MAIN
UP MAIN

15D : to Perth

DUNKELD & BIRNAM
Dunkeld (DK) 15.31
15.25 X 2 15.45
15.16 DN LP
15.21 UP LP
Up Sdgs

28.16
'SINGLE' DN
UP

19B

Row B

Miles from Perth

29 30 31 32 33 34 35 36 37 38 39 40 41 42 43 44 45 46 47 48 49 50 51 52

(Highest point on Rail Network)
DALNASPIDAL Druimuachdar
1405 ft 50.73 Summit
1484 ft (452m)

52.59

Dalnaspidal (UWC)
50.60

Red Van (UWC)
49.03

Dalnaspidal
IBS signals
Down & Up at 51.22

IBS = Intermediate
block signal

PITLOCHRY
PITLOCHRY (PT) 28.31

28.21 (PT) 28.31
28.16 UP DN 28.41
URS
28.28 Engrs

Kingswood Tunnel
(330 yards)
12.78   13.13

Tilt
Viaduct
34.72

Kings Island (UWC) 33.21
Auldclune No.3 (UWC) 34.02
34.77 UWC 35.09
(BA)

Clunes (UWC)
41.25

Pitagowan (UWC)
38.30

(Struan)
617 ft 39.50

Garry Viaduct
39.40-46

Killiecrankie
Viaduct (240 yds)
31.60-66 31.66-77

Killiecrankie
Tunnel
a = Urrard No.1 (UWC) 32.15
b = Urrard No.2 (UWC) 32.41
c = Ballentoul (UWC) 34.36

BLAIR ATHOLL
35.09
BRS
35.21
2 35.32 (11)
1 (7)

(350 ft)

(350 ft)

Tigh-Na-Geat (73)
30.56

Dalnacardoch GF
44.76

Dalnacardoch IBS signals
Down at 44.62 : Up at 45.15

19A

LMS : High. (Perth & Dunkeld) [SC 193] HGL 2

LMS : High. (Perth Jn) [SC 193] HGL 2

Row C

53 54 55 56 57 58 59 60 61 62 63 64 65 66 67 68 69 70 71 72 73 74 75 76 77

Miles from Perth

Whitebridge (UWC)
54.65

Balsporran (UWC)
54.4

DALWHINNIE
1174 ft
DALWHINNIE (DW)
58.47 58.53
X 2 58.65
1 URS
5 Up Sdgs
9 Engrs

Ben Alder (UWC)
58.30

Distillery Burn (UWC)
58.70

Cuaich (UWC)
60.41

Inchlea (UWC)
62.38

Crubenmore (UWC)
64.60

Pitmain No.1 (UWC) 69.74
Balladmyre (UWC) 70.32
Balladmyre No.2 (UWC) 70.71
Pitmain No.2 (UWC) 71.17

NEWTONMORE
68.62
(10)

68.22-27
Spey Viaduct

KINGUSSIE
745 ft
KINGUSSIE
71.43
UP DN (12) 71.27
71.60
X 2
1 (KG) 71.50
Engrs
(13)

Ralliachean (UWC) 71.27

Macraes (UWC)
72.39

Lynchat
(UWC) 73.11

Crofterton No.2
(UWC) 74.17

S Pts   N Pts
77.56
77.39
Kincraig
Loop
77.23

Aviemore
SB (AK)

Kingussie
SB (KG)

a = Balavil Burn (UWC) 73.72
b = Balavil Gates (UWC) 74.05
a b

Aviemore
(AS) (AT)

'SINGLE' DN

DOWN   UP

19B   19D

LMS : High. (Inverness & Perth Jn) [SC 193] HGL 2

Row D

78 79 80 81 82 83 84 85 86 87 88 89 90 91 92 93 94 95 96 97 98 99

Miles from Perth [SC 193] HGL 2

KINCRAIG
LOOP
77.56

AVIEMORE
AVIEMORE (AV) 83.51 Incl: (AC, AK, AM, AS, AT, AV)
83.31
83.15 DRS
83.09 UP LOOP 83.44
DN & UP
83.53 Engrs

Lynwilg No.1
(UWC) 82.31

AVIEMORE
(Speyside)

NR Bdy

STRATHSPEY RAILWAY CO. LTD.

Dalfaber (AOCL)
84.23

* = Carriage Maintenance Shed
LS

Aviemore
(AC)

'SINGLE' DN

Dulnain Viaduct
90.15-18 UP
90.16 Run
Engrs Out

CARRBRIDGE (13)
914 ft
CARRBRIDGE
90.00 N Pts
89.64 S Pts
X 2 1
Up Sdg GF

Slochd Viaduct
93.69-75

1315 ft
Slochd Summit
95.31

S Pts LOOP N Pts
95.14 95.00
95.46

Findhorn
Viaduct
98.04 98.24

Tomatin Loop
1029 ft
98.78
S Pts N Pts
98.60
98.12

Tomatin
Viaduct
98.39-44

96.18
96.03

GRANTOWN-ON-SPEY

Up
Sdgs
GF
98.65

UNDER
CONSTRUCTION

River
Dulnain

BROOMHILL
92.60

BOAT OF GARTEN
Boat of Garten North
88.43 88.51
88.49
88.22
Boat of Garten South
88.34
86.33

Aviemore
(AS) (AK)

'SINGLE' DN

Strathspey Rly : Northern Extn)

AVG LMS : High. (Inverness & Perth Jn)

19C   19E

Row Da (inset)

CAIRN GORM MOUNTAIN RLY Ltd
Balanced Funicular : Electric Traction
Length : 1,982m   Gauge : 2m (6' 6¾")

BASE STATION
635m (2,100ft)

PTARMIGAN
1097m
(3,600ft)
Tunnel
247m

a = Summer unload
b = Winter unload
c = Summer load

SHIELING
(Winter only)

Coire Cas
unload load
unload load

a b c

No official confirmation

© Peter Scott, by permission

Row E

100 101 102 103 104 105 106 107 108 109 110 111 112 113 114 115 116 117

Miles from Perth

Aviemore
(AT) (AM)

Aviemore
(AK) (A)

Aviemore
S Pts
102.71 LOOP 103.24
103.06 N Pts

Moy Loop

Aultnaslanach Vdct
103.36
(former timber structure preserved)

Aviemore
SB (AM)

Aviemore Inverness
(TCB) SC (I)

Daviot
107.14

Culloden or
River Nairn
Viaduct
110.58-111.05

CULLODEN MOOR
111.34
111.30
111.28
111.17 111.21
111.17
No.1 111.28
111.17
No.2 111.32
111.33

Culloden (CULLODEN)
111.17-111.05

Raigmore (CCTV)
143.09

A9
former
Millburn Jn
116.72 143.20
117.20

116.72 116.52
116.68
Cradiehall
Crossovers
116.56
116.45

116.37 116.52
116.22

EAST LINE' ANI 3 [SC 195]

18B : to Inverness

18B : to Nairn

'SINGLE' DN
UP MAIN
DN MAIN

19D

¥ Covered ways

ANI 3 142.71-78
HGL 2 116.72-117.01

LMS : High. (Aviemore Direct)
LMS : High. (Inverness & Perth Jn)
[SC 193] HGL 2 LMS : High. (Aviemore Direct)

December 2007

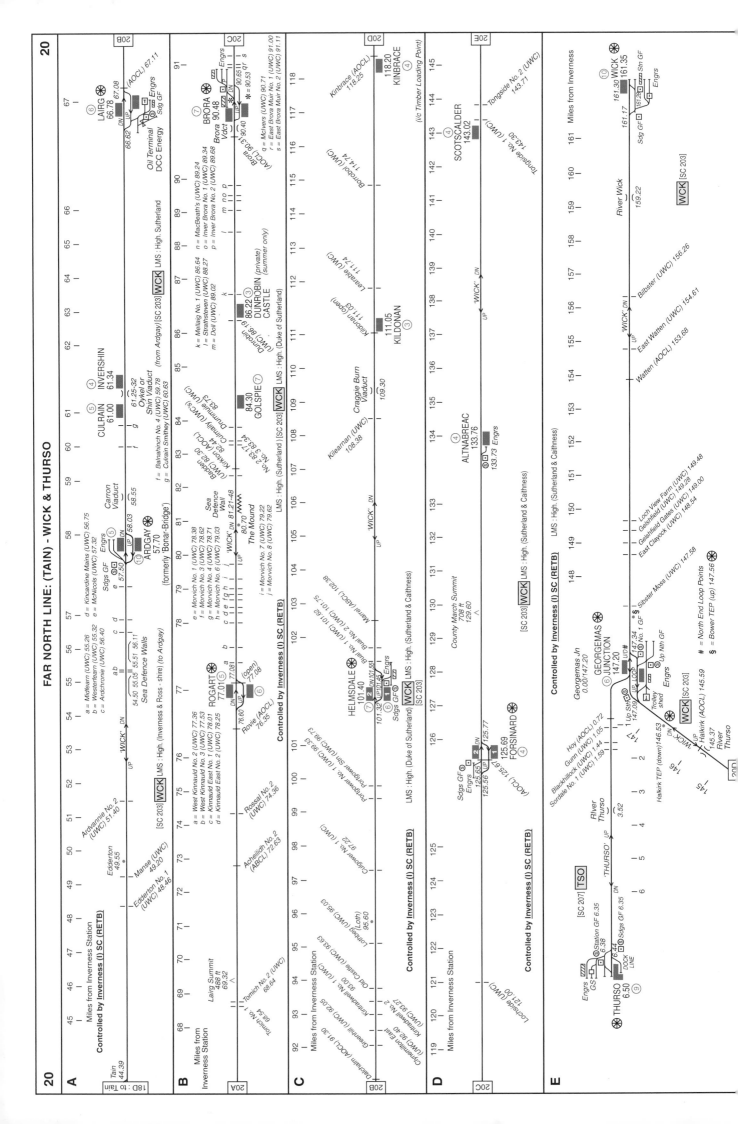

WEST HIGHLAND LINE: GARELOCHHEAD - OBAN & SPEAN BRIDGE ● MULL & WEST HIGHLAND RAILWAY

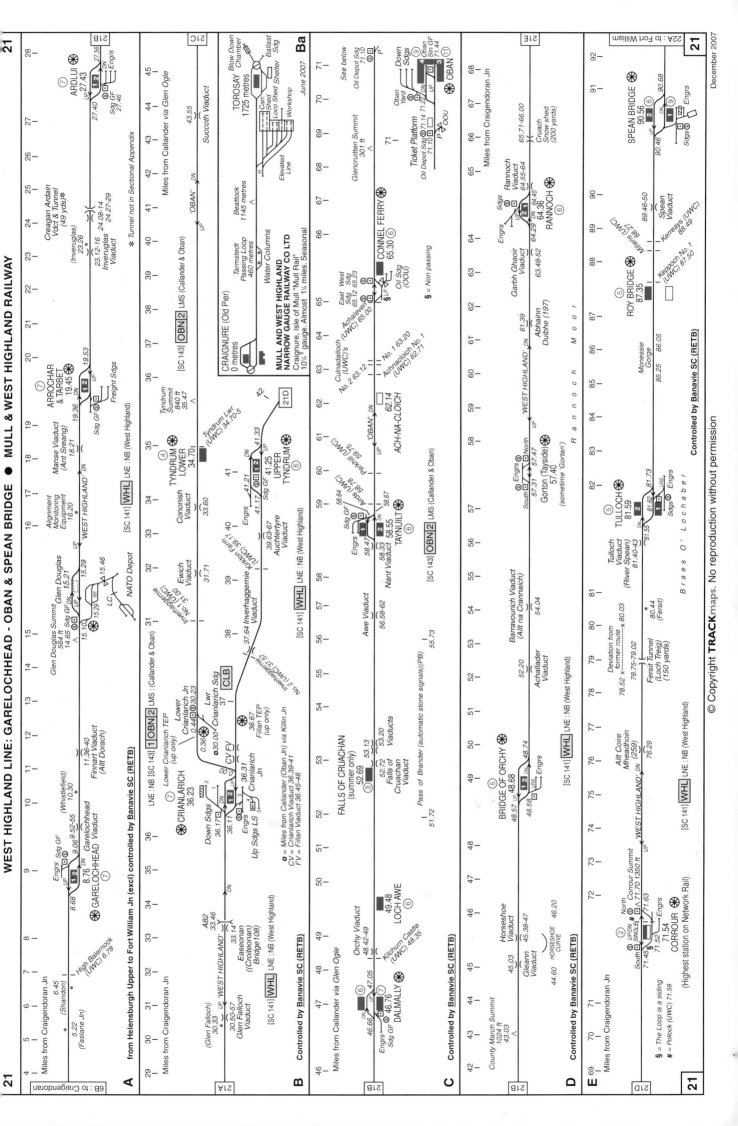

December 2007

WEST HIGHLAND LINE: FORT WILLIAM - MALLAIG ● SKYE LINE

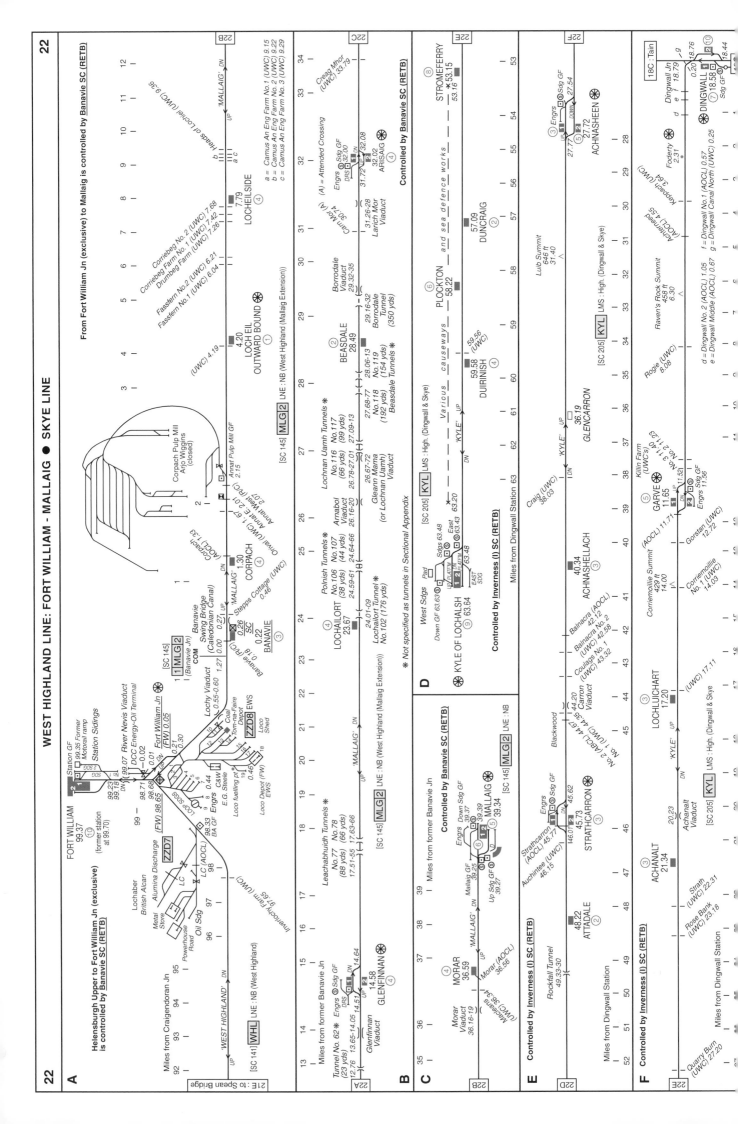

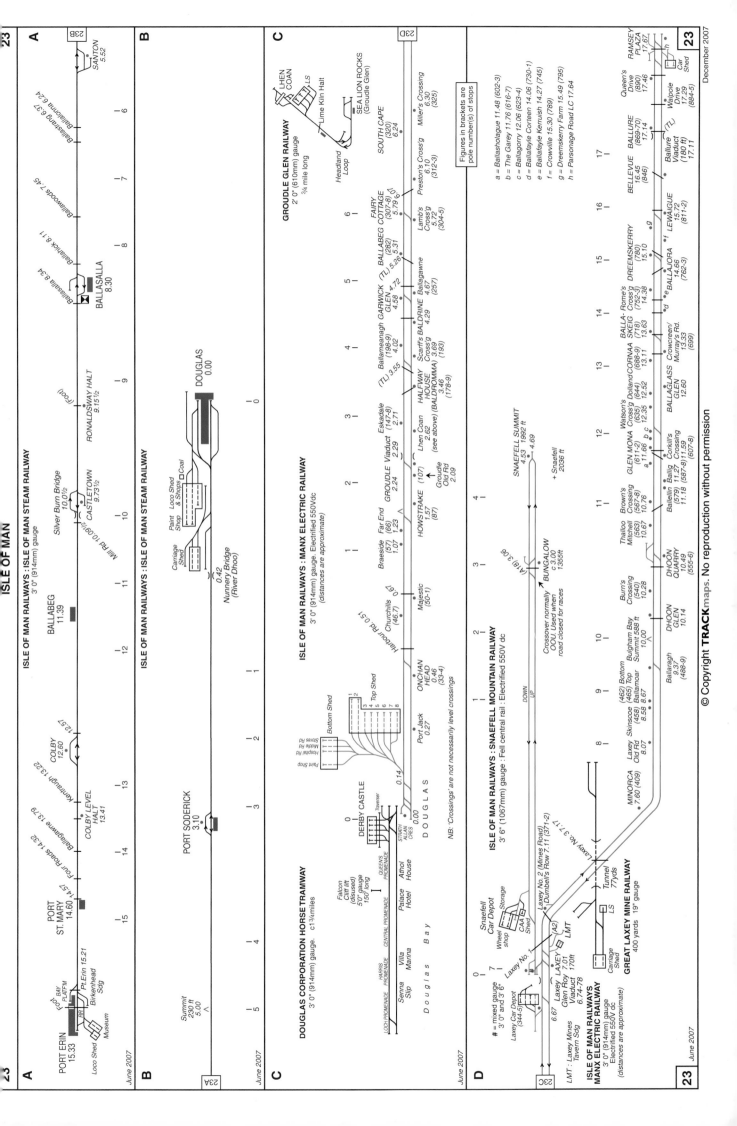

Index

In the creation of the index, the full listing of locations and assets was retained intact. They include locations of now-defunct assets (given in brackets) and level crossings and are intended to assist the reader in searching the Maps. Private and preserved railways are named in italics. At some stations, the Gaelic name is included on the station nameboard. These are indicated on the main index by an asterisk * and a separate index is provided at the end.

Haymarket Central Jn	11A
Haymarket East Jn (Duff Street Jn)	11A
Haymarket North Tunnel	11A
Haymarket South Tunnel	11A
Haymarket Sprinter Depot	11A
Haymarket West Jn	11A, 12
Heads of Lochiel LC (UWC)	22A
Heatherbell LC (CCTV)	9A
Heatherinch LC (UWC)	14C
Heathfield LC (UWC)	9A
HELENSBURGH CENTRAL	6B
HELENSBURGH UPPER*	6B
HELMSDALE*	20C
High Balernock LC (UWC)	21A
High Bank Siding GF	6B
High Bank Sidings	6B
High Street Jn	7L
High Street Tunnel	7L
HIGH STREET	7L
Hill Street Siding	3
HILLFOOT	7L
HILLHEAD (SPTE)	9B
Hillhouse Quarry (OOU)	3
HILLINGTON EAST	5A
HILLINGTON WEST	5A
Hilton Jn SB (HJ)	14C, 15C
Hilton Mills LC (UWC)	18D
Holehouse Jn GF	2C
(Hollybush)	2C
Holm Jn	4A
HOLYTOWN	8R
Holytown Jn	8R
Holywood LC (MGW)	2D
Holywood SB (HW)	2D
Horseshoe Curve	21D
Horseshoe Viaduct	21D
Hospital Mill LC (R/G)	14C
HOSPITALFIELD HALT	16Ca
HOWWOOD	5A
Hoy LC (AOCL)	20E
Hunterston Causeway LC (AOCL)	4A
Hunterston Jn	4A
HUNTLY	17D
Huntly SB (HT)	17D
Hurlford SB (HF)(Closed)	3
Hutcheon Street Tunnel	17B
Hutcheon	17B
HYNDLAND	7L
Hyndland East Jn	7L
Hyndland North Jn	7L
Hyndland West Jn	7L
IBM	5B
IBROX (SPTE)	9B
(Ibrox Jn)	5A
Inchcoonans LC (AHBC-X)	16A
Inchlea LC (UWC)	19C
Inchmagranachan No.2 LC (UWC)	19A
Inchmagranachan No.3 LC (UWC)	19A
Inchture LC (AHBC-X)	16A
Inchyra LC (AHBC)	16A
Innerleven LC (AOCL)	14B
Innerwick	11C
Innerwick Wheelchex	11C
INSCH	17C
Insch LC (MCB)	17C
Insch SB (IH)	17C
Inver Brora No.1 LC (UWC)	20B
Inver Brora No.2 LC (UWC)	20B
(Inveresk)	11A
INVERGORDON*	18D
Invergordon Distillery GF's	18D
Invergordon Distillery LC (AC)	18D
INVERGOWRIE	16A
Inverhaggernie No.1 LC (UWC)	21B
Inverhaggernie No.2 LC (UWC)	21B
Inverhaggernie Viaduct	21B
Inverkeilor SB (IR)	16C
INVERKEITHING	12, 13
Inverkeithing Car Park LC (Footpath)(R/G)	12
Inverkeithing Central Jn	12
Inverkeithing East Jn	13
Inverkeithing North Jn	13
Inverkeithing South Jn	12
Inverkeithing Tunnel	12
INVERKIP	5B
Inverkip Tunnel	5B
Inverlochty No.1 LC (UWC)	18A
Inverlochy Farm LC (UWC)	22A
INVERNESS*	18B
Inverness SC (I)	18B
Inverpeffor LC (UWC)	16C
INVERSHIN	20A
Invertiel Viaduct	13
Inveruglas Viaduct	21A
(Inveruglas)	21A
INVERURIE	17C
Inverurie SB (IE)	17C
IRVINE	4A
Irvine Viaduct	3
ISLE OF MAN TRANSPORT: ISLE OF MAN RLY	23A
ISLE OF MAN TRANSPORT: MANX ELECTRIC RLY	23C
ISLE OF MAN TRANSPORT: SNAEFELL MOUNTAIN RLY	23D
James Watt Dock	5B
Jamestown Viaduct	12
Jerviston Jn	8R
JOHNSTONE	5A
JORDANHILL	7L
Kaimes Quarry Siding	10E
Kay Park Jn	3
Keepers Bridge	2B
Keepers House LC (UWC)	18C
KEITH	17D
KEITH & DUFFTOWN RAILWAY ASSOCIATION	17E
Keith Jn SB (KJ)	17D
Keith Town	17E
KELVIN HALL (SPTE)	9B
Kelvin Viaducts	7R
KELVINBRIDGE (SPTE)	9B
KELVINDALE	7L
Kelvinhaugh Tunnel	7R
Kelvinhaugh Viaduct	7R
Kennethmont SB (KN)	17C
Kennethmont Station LC (UWC)	17C
KENNISHEAD	7R
Kennishead Viaduct	7R
Keppoch LC (UWC)	22F
Keppoch No.1 LC (UWC)	21E
KERR'S MINIATURE RAILWAY	16Ca
Kerreays LC (UWC)	21D
(Kilbirnie Jn)	4B
Kilchurn Castle LC (UWC)	21C
KILDONAN	20C
Kildonan LC (Open)	20C
Kildun No.1 LC (UWC)	18C
Kilearnan LC (UWC)	20C
Kilkerran	2B
Kilkerran SB (KK)	2B
Killiecrankie Tunnel and Viaduct	19B
Killin Farm No.2 LC (UWC)	22F
Killin Farm No.3 LC (UWC)	22F
Killoch Washery	3
(Killochan)	2B
KILMARNOCK	3
Kilmarnock Jn SB (K)	3
Kilmarnock Water Viaduct	3
KILMAURS	4B
KILPATRICK	6A
KILWINNING	4A
Kilwinning Jn	4A
KINBRACE	20C
Kinbrace LC (AOCL)	20C
Kincardine	14A
Kincardine Bridge	14A
(Kincardine Jn, Clackmannan)	15A
Kincardine Mains LC (UWC)	20A
Kincardine Viaduct	15C
Kinclair Viaduct	2B
Kinclaven LC (UWC)	19A
Kincraig Crossing	16Cb
Kincraig Loop	19C
KINGHORN	13
Kinghorn Tunnel	13
Kinghorn Viaduct	13
Kinglassie Pad	13
Kingmoor Jn	1A
Kingmoor Maintenance Depot	1A
Kingoodie Viaduct	16A
Kings Island LC (UWC)	19B
KING'S PARK	7R
KINGSKNOWE	10C
Kingsknowe (AHBC)	10C
Kingston Farm LC (UWC)	16A
KINGUSSIE*	19C
Kingussie LC (MCB)	19C
Kingussie SB (KG)	19C
Kinloss LC (AHBC)	18A
(Kinnaber Jn)	16D
KINNAIRD PARK	11A
Kinnauld East No.1 LC (UWC)	20B
Kinnauld East No.2 LC (UWC)	20B
KINNEIL HALT	12
KINNING PARK (SPTE)	9B
(Kintore)	17B
Kintradwell No.1 LC (UWC)	20C
Kintradwell No.2 LC (UWC)	20C
Kip Viaduct	5B
Kippenross Tunnel	15A
Kippenross Viaduct	15A
KIRKCALDY	13
KIRKCONNEL	2E
Kirkconnel SB (KC)	2E
KIRKHILL	7R
Kirkhill Tunnel	7R
Kirkland East	14B
Kirkland Glen Viaduct	4A
KIRKNEWTON	10E
Kirknewton LC (AHB)	10E
Kirkton Farm LC (UWC)	21B
Kirkton of Kinellar LC (UWC)	17B
Kirkton of Mailer No.2 LC (UWC)	15C
KIRKWOOD	8L
Kirkwood Viaduct	8L
Kirtle Water Viaduct (Gretna Green)	1B
Kirtle Water Viaduct (Kirtlebridge)	10A
Kirtlebridge GSP	10A
Kirton LC (AOCL)	20B
Kittybrewster	17B
(Kittybrewster)	17B
Knightswood North Jn	7L
Knightswood South Jn (former)	7L
Knightswood Tunnel	7L
Knockenjig LC (UWC)	2E
Knockshinnoch Disposal Point	2E
Knowes LC (UWC)	11B
KYLE OF LOCHALSH*	22D
LADYBANK	14C
Ladybank Jn	14D
Ladyburn Jn	5B
Ladyburn Siding	5B
Laggansarroch Viaduct	2B
Lairg LC (AOCL)	20A
Lairg Summit	20B
LAIRG*	20A
Lamberton	11C
Lamberton HABD	11C
Lamington Farm LC (UWC)	17C
Lamington	10B
Lammerlaw's Yard (Burntisland)	13
LANARK	10E
Lanark Jn	10E
LANGBANK	5A
Langloan Jn	8L
LANGSIDE	7R
(Langside Jn)	7R
LARBERT	9A, 15A
Larbert Jn	9A
Larbert North SB (LN)	15A
Larbert North	15A
Larbert Viaduct	9A
LARGS	4A
Larich Mor Viaduct	22B
Larkfield Jns	7R
LARKHALL	8R
Laurencekirk SB (LK)	16D
Laurencekirk	16D
Law Jn	8R
Leachabhuidh Tunnels	22B
LEADHILLS	10F
Learable LC (UWC)	20C
LEITH	11A
Leith Hall LC (UWC)	17C
Lentran Station LC (UWC)	18C
(Lentran)	18C
LENZIE	7L, 9A
Lenziemill Viaduct	9A
Lesmahagow Jn	8R
LEUCHARS	14C
(Leven Shipyard Jn)	6B
Leven Viaduct	6B
Levern Water Viaduct	7R
Lig Burn Viaduct	2B
Limefield Viaduct	10D
Limpetness Loop	12
Linhouse Water Viaduct (No.86)	10E
Little Genoch No.1 LC	2A
Little Genoch No.2 LC	2A
Littlemill LC (UWC)	17D
LIVINGSTON NORTH	12
LIVINGSTON SOUTH	10D
LINLITHGOW	12
LOCH AWE*	21C
Loch Eil LC (UWC)	22A
LOCH EIL OUTWARD BOUND*	22A
Loch Nam Uamh Tunnels	22B
Loch View Farm LC (UWC)	20E
Lochaber	22A
LOCHAILORT*	22B
Lochailort Tunnel	22B
LOCHEILSIDE*	22A
LOCHGELLY	13
Lochgreen Jn	3
(Lochgreen Jn)	3
Lochinver Farm LC (UWC)	18A
LOCHLUICHART	22F
Lochluichart LC (UWC)	22F
Lochmuir Jn	14C
Lochmuir Summit	14D
Lochside LC (UWC)	20D
LOCHWINNOCH	4A
Lochwinnoch Crossovers	4A
Lochy Viaduct	22A

Location	Code
LOCKERBIE	10A
Logans Road (LC (CCTV)	8R
London Road Jn	1A
Long Lyes Sidings	3
Longannet	14A
Longannet SB (LG)	14A
Longcarse LC (UWC)	15A
Longford Viaduct	4A
Longforgan SB (LF)	16A
Longley LC (UWC)	18A
LONGNIDDRY	11B
(Loth)	20C
Lothbeg LC (UWC)	20C
Lower Crianlarich Jn	21B
Lower Cullernie LC (UWC)	18B
Lows Crossing	12
Lugar Water Viaduct	3
(Lugton Jn)	4B
Lugton SB (LU)	4B
Lugton Water Viaduct	4B
Luib Summit	22E
(Lumphinnans Central)	13
Lunan Bay Viaduct	16C
(Luncarty)	19A
Lynchat LC (UWC)	19C
Lynedoch	5B
Lynedock Street Tunnel	5B
Lynwilg No.1 LC (UWC)	19D
Macleans L (UWC)	22C
Macraes LC (UWC)	19C
Main Water of Luce Viaduct	2A
MALLAIG*	22C
Manor Neuk LC (UWC)	15A
Manor Powis LC (UWC)	15A
Manse LC (UWC)	20A
Manse Viaduct	21A
Manuel	12
(Manuel)	12
Markdhu No.1 LC (UWC)	2B
MARKINCH	13
Markinch Viaduct	13
Marklach No.1 LC (UWC)	2A
Marklach No.3 LC (UWC)	2A
Markle LC (AHBC)	11B
Marrel LC (ABCL)	20C
Marshall Meadows	11C
Martinton Viaduct	1C
MARYHILL	7L
Maryhill Park Jn	7L
Maryhill Viaduct	7L
Mauchline Jn	3
Mauchline SB (MA)	3
Maxwell Goods Jn (former)	1C
MAXWELL PARK	7R
MAYBOLE	2C
Mayburgh LC	18C
McIvors LC (UWC)	20B
McNicols LC (UWC)	20A
Meadowhead	3
Mein Water Viaduct	10A
Mellaig No.1 LC (UWC)	20B
Mennock Water Viaduct	2E
(Mennock)	2E
Merryhill LC (TMO)	14A
MERRYTON	8R
Methil	14B
Methil East	14B
Methil No. 2 LC (TMO)	14B
Methil West	14B
Midcalder Jn	10D, 10E
Midfearn LC (UWC)	20A
Milburn Jn (former)	19E
Mildearie No.2 LC (UWC)	17F
Milk Water Viaduct	10A
Mill o'Keir Viaduct	15A
Millburn Jns	18B
Millens LC (UWC)	21D
Millerhill East Jn	11A
Millerhill South Jn	11A
Millerhill West Jn	11A
MILLERHILL YARD	11A
MILLIKEN PARK	5A
MILNGAVIE	7L
Milnwood Jn	8R
Milnwood Jn/Fullwood Jn	8R
Milton of Gollanfield LC (UWC)	18B
Milton of Larg No. 2 LC (UWC)	2A
Milton of Larg No.1 LC (UWC)	2A
Miltonise LC (UWC)	2B
MINNIVEY	2C
Misk (OOU)	4A
Misk Branch GF	4A
Molendinar Street Viaduct	7R
Moncrieffe Tunnel	15C, 15D
Monessie Gorge	21E
MONIFIETH	16B
Monkton Siding GF	3
Monktonhall Jn	11A
MONTROSE	16C
Montrose North SB (MN)	16C
MORAR*	22C
Morar LC (AOCL)	22C
Morar Viaduct	22C
(Morningside Jn)	8R
Morningside Road	11A
Morvich No.1 LC (UWC)	20B
Morvich No.3 LC (UWC)	20B
Morvich No.5 LC (UWC)	20B
Morvich No.6 LC (UWC)	20B
Morvich No.7 LC (UWC)	20B
Morvich No.8 LC (UWC)	20B
Moss Road LC (UWC)	6B
Mossband Jn	1B
Mossend East Jn	8R
Mossend North Jn	8L
Mossend South Jns	8R
Mossend West Jn	8R
Mossend Yards	8L
Mosset Park LC (UWC)	18A
Mossgiel Tunnel	3
Mossgiel Up IBS	3
MOSSPARK	5A
MOTHERWELL	8R
Motherwell SC (MH)(MS)(MY)	8R
Motherwell TMD (former)	8R
Moulin LC (UWC)	19B
Moulinearn	19A
Moulinearn LC (R/G)	19A
Mound Tunnels	11A
MOUNT FLORIDA	7R
MOUNT VERNON	8L
Mouse Water Viaduct	10E
Moy Loop	19E
MUIREND	7R
Muirhaouse Farm LC (UWC)(CE)	1B
Muirhead	15D
Muirhouse Jns	7R
Muirton	15D
Mulben	17E
MULL AND WEST HIGHLAND RAILWAY	21Ba
Mullben	17F
Murie LC (AHBC-X)	16A
Murthly LC	19A
Murthly LC (AHBC)	19A
MUSSELBURGH	11A
Myremill Farm LC (UWC)	2C
NAIRN*	18B
Nairn West SB (NA)	18B
Nant Viaduct	21C
NEILSTON	7R
Ness Viaduct	18B, 18C
Nethercleugh HABD	10A
(Nethercleugh)	10A
NEW CUMNOCK	2E
Newbridge Jn	12
(Newburgh)	14C
Newington	11A
NEWTON	7R, 8R
Newton East Jn	7R, 8R
Newton Jn (Newton-on-Ayr)	3
Newton Kirkhill Jn	7R
Newton of Struthers LC (UWC)	18A
Newton Street Tunnel	5B
Newton West Jn	7R
Newton, Hamilton Jn	7R
Newtonhill SB (NH)	17A
NEWTONMORE*	19C
NEWTON-ON-AYR	3
Niddrie North Jn	11A
Niddrie South Jn	11A
Niddrie West Jn	11A
Nigg LC (AHBC)	18D
NITSHILL	7R
No.1 Tunnel (Bishopston)	5A
No.2 Tunnel (Bishopston)	5A
NORTH BERWICK	11B
North Esk Viaduct	16D
NORTH OUEENSFERRY	12
North Queensferry Tunnel	12
Oakbank Viaduct	10D
OBAN*	21C
(Oban Jn)	15A
Old Castle LC (UWC)	20C
(Old Cumnock)	3
Orangefield Tunnel	5B
Orbiston Viaduct	8R
(Orbiston)	17F
Orchardbank (Perth)	15D, 16A
Orchardhall Branch (former)	12
Orchy Viaduct	21C
Ordie Viaduct	19A
Orival LC (UWC)	22A
Oxwellmains	11C
Oxwellmains HABD	11C
Oykel or Shin Viaduct	20A
Oyne LC (AHBC)	17C
PAISLEY CANAL	5A
PAISLEY GILMOUR STREET	5A
Paisley SC (P)	5A
PAISLEY ST JAMES	5A
Panbride East LC (UWC)	16B
(Parkhead North Jn)	7L
Parkhill LC (UWC)	21C
Parkhouse Jn	4A
PARTICK*	7R
PARTICK (SPTE)	9B
PATTERTON	7R
Penmanshiel	11C
PERTH	15D, 16A
Perth (New) Yard	15D
Perth SB (P)	15D
Perth South Jn	15D
Petteril Bridge Jn	1A
Philipstoun Wheelex	12
Pilmore West LC (UWC)	16A
Pinmore Tunnel	2B
(Pinmore)	2B
Pinwherry	2B
Pitagowan LC (UWC)	19B
(Pitcaple)	17C
Pitcoag LC (UWC)	16A
Pitglassie Field LC (UWC)	18C
Pitglassie North LC (UWC)	18C
Pitglassie South LC (UWC)	18C
PITLOCHRY*	19B
Pitmain No.1 LC (UWC)	19C
Pitmain No.2 LC (UWC)	19C
Pitmedden LC (R/G)	17B
Plean Jn SB (PJ)	15A
PLOCKTON*	22D
POLLOKSHAWS EAST	7R
Pollokshaws Viaduct	7R
POLLOKSHAWS WEST	7R
POLLOKSHIELDS EAST	7R
POLLOKSHIELDS WEST	7R
Polmaise Down IBS	15A
Polmaise Up IBS	15A
POLMONT	12
Polmont Jn SB	9A, 12
Polnish Tunnels	22B
Polquhap Summit	2E, 3
(Port Carlisle Branch Jn)	1A
Port Eglinton Jn	7R
Port Elphinstone	17C
PORT ERIN (IoM)	23A
PORT GLASGOW	5B
PORT SODERICK (IoM)	23B
PORT ST. MARY (IoM)	23A
Portgower No.1 LC (UWC)	20C
Portgower Station LC (UWC)	20C
PORTLETHEN	17A
Portobello	11A
Portrack Viaduct	2D
POSSILPARK & PARKHOUSE	7L
Powderhall	11A
Powderhall Branch Jn	11A
(Powfoot)	1C
PRESTONPANS	11A
PRESTWICK TOWN	3
PRIESTHILL & DARNLEY	7R
Princes Pier (Greenock)	5B
Princes Street Gardens (Edinburgh)	11A
Princes Street Viaduct	16A
Princess Street LC (AOCL)	4A
Pye Road LC (UWC)	16A
Quarry Burn LC (UWC)	22F
Queen Street High Level Tunnel	7L
QUEEN'S PARK	7R
Quintinshill	1B
Quioggs No.1 LC (UWC)	15B
Raigmore LC (CCTV)	18B, 19E
Raith's Farm (Dyce)	17C
RANNOCH*	21D
Rannoch Viaduct	21D
Ratho Viaduct	12
(Ratho)	12
Raven's Rock Summit	22F
Ravenstruther	10E
Red Van LC (UWC)	19B
Redcraig Viaduct	3
Redford Jn	13
RENTON	6B
Reston	11C
Rhu	6B
(Rhu)	6B
Riccarton	3
Rigg LC (UWC)(CE)	1B
River Ayr Viaduct	3
River Carron Viaduct	2E

Gaelic names

At some stations, the Gaelic name is included on the station nameboard. These are indicated on the main index by an asterisk * and the index below describes the Gaelic name.

Achnasheen	Achadh na sine
Ardlui	Ard Laoigh
Arisaig	Arasaig
Arrochar and Tarbet	An Tairbeart
Aviemore	An Aghaidh Mhor
Banavie	Banbhaidh
Beasdale	Biasdail
Beauly	A'Mhanachainn
Blair Atholl	Blàr Athall
Bridge of Orchy	Drochaid Urchaidh
Carrbridge	Drochaid Chàrr
Connel Ferry	Aigeag a' Chonghail
Corpach	A'Chorpaich
Corrour	Coire Odhar
Crianlarich	A'Chrion Làraich
Culrain	Cui Raoin
Dalmally	Dail Mhàilidh
Dalmuir	Dail Mhoire
Dalwhinnie	Dail Chuinnidh
Dingwall	Inbhirpheofharain
Dumbarton Central	Dùn Breatainn
Dunkeld and Birnam	Dùn Chailleann is Braonan
Falls of Cruachan	Easa Chruachain
Fort William	An Gearasdan
Garelochhead	Ceann a'Gheàrrloch
Garve	Gairbh
Glasgow Queen Street	Stràid na Banrighinn
Gleneagles	Gleann Eagas
Glenfinnan	Gleann Fhionnainn
Goispie	Goillspidh

Helensburgh Upper	Baile Eilidh
Helmsdale	Bun illidh
Invergordon	Inbhirghordain
Inverness	Inbhir Nis
Kingussie	Ceann a' Ghiùthsaich
Kyle of Lochalsh	Caol Loch Aillse
Lairg	Luirg
Loch Awe	Loch Obha
Loch Eil Outward Bound	Loch Iall
Lochailort	Loch Ailleart
Locheilside	Taobh Loch Iall
Mallaig	Malaig
Morar	Mòrar
Nairn	Inbhir Narann
Newtonmore	Bail Ùr an t-Slèibh
Oban	An t-Oban
Partick	Partaig
Pitlochry	Balle Chloichridh
Plockton	Ploc Loch Aillse
Rannoch	Raineach
Rogart	Sgire Raoird
Roy Bridge	Drochaid Ruaidh
Spean Bridge	Drochaid an Aonachain
Strathcarron	Srath Carrann
Tain	Baile Dhubhthaich
Taynuilt	Taigh an Uillt
Tulloch	An Tulach
Tyndrum Lower	Taigh an Droma Iarach
Upper Tyndrum	Taigh an Droma Uarach

Yards to Chains Conversion Table

As applied within Network Rail Scotland. Yardages are rounded to the nearest ten.

Yards	Chains	Yards	Chains	Yards	Chains	Yards	Chains	Yards	Chains
20		420	19	810	37	1210	55	1610	73
40	2	440	20	840	38	1230	56	1630	74
70	3	460	21	860	39	1250	57	1650	75
90	4	480	22	880	40	1280	58	1670	76
110	5	510	23	900	41	1300	59	1690	77
130	6	530	24	920	42	1320	60	1720	78
150	7	550	25	950	43	1340	61	1740	79
180	8	570	26	970	44	1360	62		
200	9	590	27	990	45	1390	63		
220	10	620	28	1010	46	1410	64		
240	11	640	29	1030	47	1430	65		
260	12	660	30	1060	48	1450	66		
290	13	680	31	1080	49	1470	67		
310	14	700	32	1100	50	1500	68		
330	15	730	33	1120	51	1520	69		
350	16	750	34	1140	52	1540	70		
370	17	770	35	1170	53	1560	71		
400	18	790	36	1190	54	1580	72		

ENGINEERS LINE REFERENCES

The extent of each ELR is indicated by the page references. Where both boundaries appear on the same page, only one reference is given. Where one appears in another Track Diagram book, the reference is in the format Book:page.

Code	Description	Pages
ANI	Aberdeen - Inverness	17A, 18B
ANN	Newton Jn - Mauchline Jn (via Annbank)	3
ARG	Rutherglen Central Jn - Finnieston Jn (Argyle line)	7R
ARH	Ardrossan Holm Jn - Ardrossan Harbour	4A
AYH	Ayr Harbour branch (Newton Jn and Falkland Yard - Ayr Harbour)	3
AYR	Glasgow Central (Bridge Jn) - Ayr	7R, 3
BAK	Barassie Jn - Kilmarnock Stn Jn	3
BCH	Dalreoch Jn - Balloch	6B
BGD	Alves Jn - Burghead	18A
BID	Burntisland Dock Jn - Burntisland Dock	13
BRD	Shields Jn - Terminus Jn (Burma Road)	7R
BSN	Stainton - Carlisle Yard (Brunthill Branch sdg)	1A
BWL	Glencraig Jn - Bowhill Washery (OOU)	13
BYL	Dubbs Jn - Byrehill Jn	4A
CBC	Carnforth N Jn - Carlisle S Jn via Whitehaven	1A, 4:29C
CBD	Sighthill East Jn - Garnqueen N Jn (Cumbernauld line)	7R, 9A
CDC	Ladybank Jn - Hilton Jn (via Clatchard Craig)	14C
CGJ	Crewe - Carlisle via Penrith	1A, 4:29C
CKT	Craiglockhart Jn - Slateford Jn	11A
CLB	Crianlarich Lower sdg - Crianlarich Lower Jn	21B
CLY	Larkfield Jn - Shields Jns (Clydesdale line)	7R
CMS	Carmuirs West Jn - Carmuirs East Jn	9A
CNC	Cathcart N Jn - Cathcart E Jn	7R
CND	Cardonald Jn - Deanside	5A
CNL	Shields Jn - Paisley Canal (Canal line)	7R, 5A
CON	Container Base Jn - Greenock Container Depot	5B
COS	Coltness Works - Garriongill Jn	8R
CPH	Craigentinny, Powderhall Branch Jn - Powderhall	11A
CRE	Capledrae - Redford Jn (Westfield branch)	13
CRN	Elbowend Jn - Crombie (Charlestown branch)	14A
CSN	Cowlairs E Jn - Cowlairs N Jn	7L
CSP	Carstairs Station Jn - Carstairs E Jn	10E
CTC	Cathcart Circle (Muirhouse Central Jn - Muirhouse Central Jn)	7R
CWH	Inverkeithing Central Jn - Thornton S Jn via Cowdenbeath	13
DFN	Keith Jn - Dufftown	17E
DMY	Dalmeny Jn - Winchburgh Jn	12
ECA	Edinburgh, Haymarket East Jn - Carstairs South Jn (via Cobbinshaw)	11A, 10E
ECM	East Coast Main line (London, Kings Cross - Edinburgh, Waverley)	2:23B, 11A
ECN	East Coast Main North (Edinburgh, Waverley - Aberdeen)	11A, 17A
EGM	Edinburgh and Glasgow Main (Edinburgh, Waverley - Glasgow, Queen St, via Falkirk High)	11A, 7L
EGS	Midcalder Jn - Uddingston Jn (Edinburgh - Glasgow via Shotts)	10D, 8R
EKE	Busby Jn - East Kilbride	7R
ETC	Edinburgh, Waverley - Carlisle Canal Jn (Waverley route)	1A
GBK	Muirhouse S Jn - Kilmarnock GB & K Jn (Glasgow, Barrhead and Kilmarnock Jt)	7R, 3
GGE	Gorgie Jn - Haymarket West Jn	11A
GHE	Gartsherrie S Jn - Gartcosh Jn	9A
GHL	Greenhill Upper Jn - Greenhill Lower Jn	9A
GIF	Lugton Jn - Giffen	4B
GIR	Girvan Jn - Girvan Goods (OOU)	2B
GMH	Grangemouth Jn - Grangemouth Harbour	12
GNE	Gunnie Yard - Coatbridge Sunnyside Jn (OOU)	8L
GNN	Greenburn Jn - Greenburn Opencast	2E
GOU	Paisley, Wallneuk Jn - Gourock	5A, 5B
GSW	Kilmarnock GB & K Jn - Gretna Jn (Glasgow & South Western)	3, 1B
GUD	Aberdeen South Jn - Guild Street	17A
HGL	Highland line (Perth - Inverness via Carrbridge)	15D, 18B
HIL	Shewalton Moss GF - Hillhouse Quarry (OOU)	3
HMN	Hamilton branch (Motherwell Jn - Newton, Hamilton Jn via Hamilton)	8R
HST	Glasgow, High Street Jn - Shields Jns (City Union)	7R
HUN	Hunterston Jn - Hunterston LL branch	4A
HYD	Hyndland North Jn - Hyndland West Jn	7L
IGE	Inverkeithing E Jn - Inverkeithing N Jn	13
INS	Inverness Harbour Branch	18B
IRE	Irvine Depot - Irvine Jn	4A
JVN	Jerviston, Ravenscraig Sdg	8R
JWT	Ladyburn Jn - James Watt Dock (OOU)	5B
KCH	Annbank Jn - Killoch Washery	3
KHL	Newton, Kirkhill Jn - Cathcart West Jn (Kirkhill line)	7R
KMG	Kingmoor Jn - Mossband Jn via Goods lines	1A, 1B
KNE	Kincardine (Clackmannan) Jn - Charlestown Jn via Elbowend Jn	15A, 14A
KSH	Bank Jn - Knockshinnoch Disposal Point	2E
KYL	Dingwall Jn - Kyle of Lochalsh	22F, 22D
LFS	Larkfield Jns - Muirhouse S Jn	7R
LGS	Kilwinning Jn - Largs	4A
LHS	Portobello Jn - Leith South	11A
LNK	Lanark Jn - Lanark	10E
LNR	Rutherglen Central Jn/Strathclyde Jn - London Road (eol)	7R
LRK	Haughead Jn - Larkhall	8R
LYE	Smithy Lye Through siding (Cook St - Shields Road)	7R
MDE	Mossend South Jn - Mossend E Jn	8R
MDN	Mossend N Jn - Mossend E Jn	8R
MDW	Mossend S Jn - Mossend W Jn	8R
MEN	Muirhouse S Jn - Eglinton St. Jn	7R
MGE	Westerton Jn - Milngavie	7L
MHL	Monktonhall Jn - Millerhill East Jn and Millerhill Yard	11A
MHY	Niddrie West Jn - Niddrie S Jn	11A
MLA	Maryhill Park Jn - Anniesland	11A
MLE	Millerhill S Jn - Millerhill E Jn	11A
MLG	Fort William Jn - Mallaig (Mallaig Extension)	22A, 22C
MRL	Cowlairs W Jn - Knightswood N Jn (Maryhill line)	7L
MSK	Stevenston - Misk ICI (OOU)	4A
MTL	Thornton N Jn - Methil	13, 14B
MYO	Mossend Down Yard	8L
MYP	Mossend Up Yard	8L
NBE	Newbridge Jn - Bathgate	12
NBK	Drem Jn - North Berwick	11B
NDE	Niddrie North Jn – Bmillerhill South Jn	11A
NEC	Newcastle - Carlisle S Jn	1A, 4:29C
NEM	Drumgelloch - Helensburgh via Queen St LL and Singer (North Electric Main line)	8L, 7, 6B
NNH	Cathcart West Jn - Neilston	7R
OBN	Crianlarich Upper Jn - Oban	21B, 21C
OCL	Fouldubs Jn - Alcan siding (Orchardhall branch)	12
PMT	Polmont Jn - Larbert Jn	12, 9A
PNS	Cowlairs S Jn - Sighthill W Jn (Cowlairs Chord line)	7L
RCB	Rutherglen E Jn - Coatbridge Jn (Carmyle line)	7R, 8L
RHD	Inverkeithing S Jn - Rosyth Dockyard	12
RIC	Kay Park Jn - Riccarton	3
RNC	Rutherglen W Jn - Rutherglen N Jn	3
RSL	Langloan Jn - Whifflet N Jn via Rosehall Jn	8L
RSW	Welsh's Bridge Jn - Rose Street Jn	18B
RVS	Clydebank Jn - Dalmuir Riverside (Riverside line) (OOU)	6A
SAA	Stirling Middle Jn - Alloa & Kincardine (Clackmannan Jn)	15A, 14A
SCG	Carlisle Bog Jn - Forks Jn	1A
SCM	Motherwell - Dundee Central Jn via Perth (Scottish Central Main)	8L, 16B
SDG	Bogside Jn - Snodgrass ICI (OOU)	4A
SGN	Cowlairs W Jn - Bellgrove Jn (Springburn line)	7L
SHR	Wishaw Central Jn - Shieldmuir North Jn	8R
STN	Stranraer Harbour Jn - Stranraer Town	2A
STR	Ayr - Stranraer	3, 2A
SUB	Portobello Jn - Haymarket Central Jn (Surburban line)	11A
SYE	Whifflet South Jn - Sunnyside Jn	8L
TNW	Thornton W Jn - Thornton N Jn	13
TSO	Georgemas Jn - Thurso	20E
TSS	Muirhouse Central Jn - Terminus Jn	7R
WAT	Dalrymple Jn - Chalmerston (Waterside branch)	2C
WCK	Inverness stn - Wick	18B, 20E
WCM	West Coast Main Line (Carlisle - Glasgow Central)	1A, 7R
WHL	Craigendoran Jn - Fort William (West Highland line)	6B, 22A
WRO	Kittybrewster Jn - Waterloo	17B
WWD	Law Jn - Holytown Jn	8R
WYS	Wemyss Bay Jn - Wemyss Bay	5B
YKR	Hyndland East Jn - Dalmuir Park Jn via Yoker	7L, 6A
ZZA1	Mauchline Jn sidings	3
ZZA2	Ayr EWS Depot	3
ZZA3	Roche Sidings, Dalry	4A
ZZA4	Barassie Overhead Line Depot	3
ZZA5	Meadowhead Paper Mill sidings, Irvine	3
ZZA6	Shewalton Engr's Coup sidings	3
ZZA7	Kilmarnock, Hunslet Barclay sidings	3
ZZA8	Engr's Plant Depot, Kilmarnock	3
ZZA9	Springburn Works sidings (Railcare)	7L
ZZB1	Shields Depot sidings	7R
ZZB2	Corkerhill CSMD sidings	5A
ZZB3	Haymarket Sprinter Depot	11A
ZZB4	Eastfield sidings	7L
ZZB7	Long Lyes sidings, Kilmarnock	3
ZZB8	Fouldubs (Grangemouth)	12
ZZC1	Gunnie Cement Terminal (OOU)	8L
ZZC2	Hunterston HL sidings	4A
ZZC5	Shettleston Plant Depot sidings	8L
ZZC6	TDG sidings, Grangemouth	12
ZZC7	Rutherglen Training School sidings	7R
ZZC8	Motherwell TMD	8R
ZZC9	Mossend Up Yard	8L
ZZD1	Mossend Down Yard	8L
ZZD2	Coatbridge Container Base sidings	8L
ZZD4	Rutherglen P/Way Depot sidings	7R
ZZD5	Polmadie Carriage Servicing Depot sidings	7R
ZZD7	BAC sidings, Fort William	22A
ZZD8	Fort William Yard	22A
ZZE4	Lafarge sidings, Uddingston	8R
ZZE9	Kilwinning station Up sidings	4A
ZZF2	Dumbarton Engr's sidings	6B
ZZF3	Ayr Townhead EMU sidings	3
ZZF4	Sighthill Jn - Springburn Works boundary	7L
ZZF5	ICI sidings, Stevenston (OOU)	4A

Notes